Com
th   y

Tech   and
prep   ption

Berni

with m
edition by Judith Cipolla,
Dorothy Benson McGown and
Mary Anne Yanulis

BAAF
ADOPTION
& FOSTERING

Published by
British Association for Adoption & Fostering
(BAAF)
Saffron House
6–10 Kirby Street
London EC1N 8TS
www.baaf.org.uk

Charity registration 275689 (England and Wales) and SC039337 (Scotland)

© BAAF, 2009

British Library Cataloguing in Publication Data
A catalogue record for this book is available from the British Library

ISBN 978 1 905664 65 8

Project management by Shaila Shah, Director of Publications, BAAF

Photographs sourced from www.istockphoto.com unless otherwise indicated
All photographs posed by models

Designed and typeset by Andrew Haig Associates

Printed in Great Britain by The Lavenham Press

Trade distribution by Turnaround Publisher Services, Unit 3, Olympia Trading Estate, Coburg Road, London N22 6TZ

BAAF is the leading UK-wide membership organisation for all those concerned with adoption, fostering and child care issues.

For all of the children – my teachers –
who invite me to play

Thank you, especially to those
referenced in the book

Acknowledgments

To Keith, Chris and Josie – I know I am blessed

To Shaila and Jo – much respect

The author

Berni Stringer is a Trainer Consultant with BAAF Midlands and an Associate Lecturer with the Open University.

She is a social worker and supervisor who, over the last three decades, has worked with children and their families and carers in residential and field work where she has been a manager and practitioner. She is experienced in family therapy and solution-focused brief therapy.

She is a practising non-directive play therapist and works predominantly with children in care who have experienced harm and for whom relationships with adults cause anxiety and fear, thereby threatening their options for permanency.

She has also co-authored guides on understanding children's behaviour and on anger management in children.

Note

This edition of *Communicating through Play* updates and expands on an edition published by BAAF in 1992. That edition, also titled *Communicating through Play: Techniques for assessing and preparing children for adoption*, was written by Judith Cipolla, Dorothy Benson McGown and Mary Ann Yanulis, and was a UK edition of a book first published in the USA.

This current edition contains much of the material originally published in 1992, which Berni Stringer has revised and added to. At the time, the original authors worked for an agency called Spaulding for Children, which is a multi-faceted organisation that provides help to children who wait the longest for permanency and offers support services for their adoptive, foster and kinship families. It is a private, non-profit child welfare agency and is based in the USA.

Contents

Introduction

The first edition of *Communicating through Play* was originally developed by the Adoption Assessment and Preparation Project at New York Spaulding for Children. Over a period of three years, project staff focused on assessing and preparing 22 children ranging in age from five to 15. Many of the techniques used were taught to Spaulding staff by Agnes (Nessie) Bayley, the supervising consultant on the project. The Spaulding Adoption Assessment and Preparation Project began with several assumptions about child development and about the activities of the worker in assessing and preparing children for adoption. These assumptions were based on attachment theory and on clinical experience. They informed the casework with individual children described in the first UK edition, which was published in 1992.

The book has been updated and revised to include an overview of some recent legislative and procedural changes, an exploration of the challenges of working within limited resources and timescales, and takes account of the changing roles and responsibilities of social workers who case manage the processes in the steps to achieving permanency for children.

Building on the work, this book also explores the importance of non-directive child-centred play and how these skills can be used by workers and also parents and carers to accelerate the attachment relationship.

Some of the original text has been preserved to maintain the key messages of the original work and the book retains its original aim, which was to:

- help adoption workers develop a larger repertoire of techniques for assessing and preparing children for adoption;

- help workers become more skilled at observing and encouraging attachment behaviour in their own interactions with children and use these observations to communicate assessment findings to adoptive parents and, in so doing, to help parents understand and use these findings in their day-to-day parenting;

- develop an ability to engage with children in nurturing and playful ways to explore and experience their strategies for forming relationships with adults;

- consider how the relationship between children and their carers can be enhanced through the play process and to explore the nature and purpose of play in child development; and

- explore how children can be helped to heal through play.

The importance of children's rights has moved up the childcare agenda in recent years. An important way of involving children is to seek their views and opinions and, where possible, to act on them. Increasingly, the importance of listening to children as a means of safeguarding them is being understood. Where major decisions are being made about their lives, children have a right to be involved, whatever their age or ability, and to communicate their needs. It is incumbent on children's social workers and/or carers to develop knowledge of child development, a commitment to children's rights and the skills to communicate. An essential skill is the ability to play. Research in attachment theory, brain development and the power of play has added to our knowledge and understanding of the central issues for children separated from their parents and informs ways of being and interacting with children to protect and promote their well-being.

There is increasing awareness that children who have endured separation from birth parents, multiple transitions in the care system, isolation and lack of certainty, layered on abuse and neglect from those whose duty it is to love and protect them, present unique challenges to their corporate parents, requiring particular skills and self-awareness on the part of carers to contain them. Children with these experiences need a delicate balance of nurturing and boundaries so that they can heal and thrive and modify or change the strategies for safety which they may have developed.

A number of scandals have rocked the care system over recent years, which have raised awareness that children in care are some of the most vulnerable. Those children who experience racism or isolation are even more vulnerable and, as the number of children and young people seeking safety and asylum increases, our resources, both economic and personal, are increasingly stretched. We are challenged to hear the unspeakable from children in our communities and even more so to help them heal.

The *Every Child Matters* agenda in England and Wales requires that we ensure children are healthy, safe, have the capacity to enjoy and achieve and eventually grow up to be citizens who make a positive contribution and achieve economic wellbeing (*www.everychildmatters.gov. uk/children/*).

Agencies are increasingly aware that protecting children goes beyond the requirement to keep them safe. The first step in this process of protection and promotion is to listen to children, hear what they have to say and learn to communicate with *all* children, particularly those who have been harmed by abuse, loss, separation and poor decision-making.

This book aims to describe a variety of verbal and non-verbal techniques which can assist the adult and the child in making this journey in their relationship with each other. Your creativity, empathy, reflection and insight will provide the necessary fuel for the ongoing sustenance of the child in their journey. Your confidence in allowing the child to set the pace and the direction will be the first step in your child's path towards integration and wholeness.

The structure of the book

Chapters 1 and 2 present the theoretical background on which the use of play techniques for child assessment and preparation is based. Central to Spaulding's work is the concept of the arousal–relaxation cycle, and this is discussed within the wider concept of attachment theory. A discussion is included of the many developments in recent years that have assisted our understanding of play as a means of communicating with children about the things that worry them. There is further discussion about how play in the relationship between carer and child can encourage and amplify attachment-seeking and needing behaviours and responses. Chapter 2 provides an overview of legislative requirements pertaining to the child's assessment.

Chapters 3 to 6 use case examples to illustrate a variety of assessment and preparation techniques, including methods for developing rapport, enhancing the child's sensory development, engaging the child in play activities about family memories, and beginning traditional life story work. These chapters include a discussion of the importance of valuing the child's individuality and heritage.

Chapter 7 describes how filial therapy can be used to enhance the relationship between children and their parents or carers.

1 Attachment:
The arousal–relaxation cycle and implications for permanence

Trust and attachment in child development

Attachment has been defined in a number of different ways over the last half century. Kennell *et al* (1976) defined attachment as 'an affectional bond between two individuals that endures through space and time and serves to join them emotionally'. By maintaining physical proximity to one who is stronger, children may receive protection provided by the attachment figure. What is generally agreed is that early attachment relationships between infants and their caregivers lead to the formation of mental representations of the self, others, and of the self in relation to others. *The Attachment Handbook for Foster Care and Adoption* (Schofield and Beek, 2007) provides a comprehensive and accessible account of core attachment concepts with reference to

real-life case scenarios, illustrated by vivid case examples.

According to Erikson (1963), one of the foundations of normal child development is "basic trust". Trust is the confidence which develops from the 'consistency, continuity, and sameness of experience' provided by the infant's carer. Basic trust results in a sense of trust in oneself and one's capacities. Ancient wisdom tells us that the mother–baby relationship is primary and the ages of 0–3 years are critical in the development of babies and infants.

Developments in the use of magnetic resonance imaging (MRI) scans and neurobiology give us a definition of attachment as a biological process which provides the neural pathways which determine a view of the world and relationships and one's sense of self within it, and the ability to regulate our own emotions and function in a more satisfying way in relationships. Children

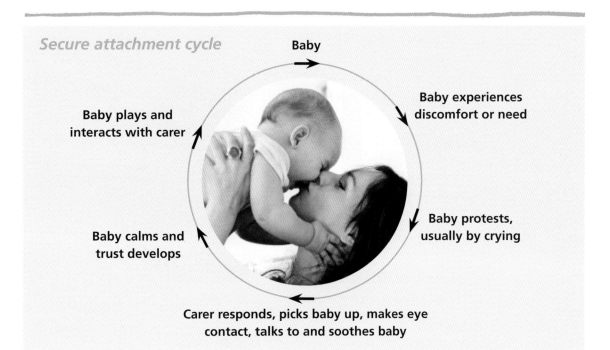

Secure attachment cycle

Baby

Baby experiences discomfort or need

Baby protests, usually by crying

Carer responds, picks baby up, makes eye contact, talks to and soothes baby

Baby calms and trust develops

Baby plays and interacts with carer

who have been neglected and abused, as many children in the care system have been, frequently have a distorted sense of trust in others and in themselves. The important work of Cozzolini (2006), Schore (see *The Thinking Body*, 2001), and Siegel (1999) provides evidence that children who have been hurt by neglect and abuse can heal and develop satisfying and meaningful relationships in the future, when supported in caring and attuned relationships. Cutting-edge science tells us that the prenatal period and early months are imperative in brain development, which may have life-long implications for our sense of well-being. In a nutshell, good care is essential to developing our emotional life so that we can experience and grow into who we are.

How can this occur?

Fahlberg's (1994) arousal–relaxation cycle illustrates "good enough" parent–child interactions leading to trust and attachment.

According to Fahlberg, the infant (or older child) experiences tension until a need is felt, such as a need for food or attention. The child shows their discomfort or need by crying or an expression of distress. When the need is consistently met by the parent, who soothes the baby by picking them up, making eye contact and touching, the child soothes and can subsequently rest, relax and play. The timely response of the adult creates the predictability which is so important in the

development of trust and attachment and self-regulation. This cycle is repeated many times in a day, week and month, as the child develops a sense of the world as a safe place where needs are responded to. However, this is only one part of the process. The other part is the sense of security and self-esteem as being lovable and cared for, which develops too. Each time the child experiences good care, neural pathways in the brain are strengthened and the blueprint for future relationships evolves and develops.

Disturbances in trust and attachment

In a situation in which care is inconsistent or poor, or the parent is overwhelmed, the cycle becomes disrupted. The infant signals a need which is met inconsistently or not met, causing the baby to become more dysregulated. If the carer then responds with anger or their own distress, the child has little option but to rage to the point of being inconsolable and/or to give up. The child eventually learns that it is unsafe to signal a need and becomes apathetic or depressed.

Where an infant's needs are met with anger or hostility, the child is in a paradox of having to seek comfort from the very person who has become extremely frightening, so the world is experienced as unfriendly and hostile and the child experiences the self as unloved and unlovable. Hyper-vigilance and avoidance may

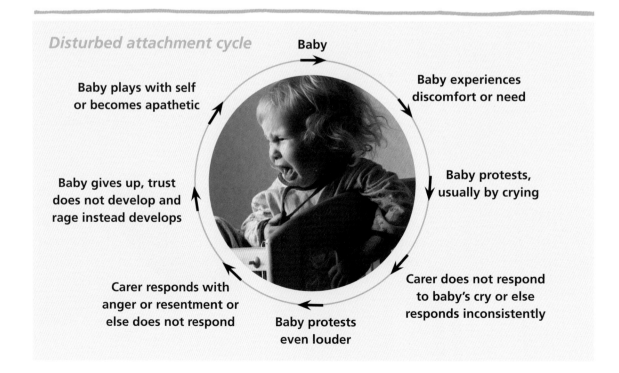

Disturbed attachment cycle

Baby

Baby experiences discomfort or need

Baby protests, usually by crying

Carer does not respond to baby's cry or else responds inconsistently

Baby protests even louder

Carer responds with anger or resentment or else does not respond

Baby gives up, trust does not develop and rage instead develops

Baby plays with self or becomes apathetic

become functional strategies for a child in an abusive or neglectful caregiving relationship. Later, when nurturing care is freely available and abundant, the same strategies become millstones which create tension, distress and feelings of rejection for all concerned.

Disturbances in the arousal–relaxation cycle lead to the inability to self-soothe or self-regulate, which means that, under stress, children become out of control and cannot accept care from a primary carer to soothe or support them – proximity to adults has become dangerous. Children with these experiences cannot use their carers as a secure base. Bowlby (1982) emphasised the role that the earliest relationships play in support of exploration and competence as the child increases the distance between himself and his attachment figure to the point that the parent or carer can be temporarily left, enabling the child to explore the world and play with a degree of independence.

When working well, the arousal–relaxation cycle will provide the child with experiences of emotion regulation, the experience of "feeling felt" in a synchrony with her carer, and feeling relaxed to explore and play. The carer is in fact the child's first "big toy" (Auerbach, 1998).

Disturbances in attachment and in the arousal–relaxation cycle, as described by Fahlberg, can lead to a multitude of difficulties in development, including the capacity to self-regulate, make and maintain relationships, problem-solve and trust self and others.

Building trust and attachment in adoption and permanence

One of the ways in which adoptive families can help their children to build trust and repair disrupted attachments is by changing the cycle of distancing behaviour to a cycle of positive interaction. When distancing patterns are apparent, parents can learn to prevent or interrupt the behaviour which might otherwise form barriers between the adult and the child. If the parent can meet the child's needs immediately – as they would do with an infant or very young

child – and manage this consistently for as long as needed, the child begins to trust in the constancy of the adult. How to do this in play will be discussed further in Chapter 7.

Consistent and predictable responsiveness to physical and emotional needs is important, regardless of the child's age, although it is difficult to practise with school-age children who are proud of their independence. Nevertheless, it is essential in helping them to develop security and trust.

Activities which promote trust and attachment, according to Fahlberg, can be as simple as accompanying the child to doctors' appointments or being available to share exciting or frightening events with the child. In these and similar situations, parents can be present during the arousal and the relaxation periods, providing comfort and building closeness. However, the challenge can be an enormous one and the experience of living with a mistrustful, anxious and highly aroused child can be draining, as this parent describes:

> Initially on arriving in our home, Arron presented as an independent little boy who wasn't overly keen on being touched or hugged. We first noticed this when trying to cuddle him – that he only tolerated it for approximately three seconds, before we had to put him down, so he could continue with whatever activity he was doing.

Arron, at 14 months old and moving into his permanent family, had learned to manage proximity with adults. He had learned to be very self-sufficient.

How can play help?

Play is explicitly recognised in the United Nations Convention of the Rights of the Child (UNCRC) article 31, which states: 'Parties recognise the right of the child to rest and leisure to engage in play and recreational activities appropriate to the age of the child and to participate freely in cultural life and the arts.' Play is central to children's development and is essential for supporting children in reaching social, emotional and cognitive milestones. The arousal–relaxation process experienced regularly in play helps them to manage stress, develop emotional regulation and become more resilient (Ginsburg, 2006).

Abused and neglected children and young people in care have many gaps in experience which limit their emotional, social and intellectual growth. Workers and parents can come closer to understanding these young people by thinking of them as children much younger than their chronological age, whose learned skills for self-protection and relationships are no longer functional in the context of good care. Adoptive parents can teach their children much about the world. The teaching works best when the child is relaxed enough to absorb it, and children are most relaxed and open to learning and experience in play.

The feelings experienced in play are many and varied. You may remember how immersed you became in your own play as a child. The arousal–relaxation cycle is experienced repeatedly! Now think of a child playing with toy soldiers. He will experience a mix of fear, anger, satisfaction, pride, frustration, boredom and exhilaration. During this time, the child becomes aroused, self-soothes and relaxes over and over again. However, when children play, adults tend to leave them alone! The cycle can be missed. Play witnessed by a caring and interested adult, who contains the child's anxiety, celebrates success and shares relaxed moments, can lead to healing and growth. This can replicate the arousal–relaxation cycle, which is so important in developing a child's understanding of experiences and the capacity to self-regulate.

Assessing and preparing children for permanence and adoption

Social workers and foster carers are key players in preparing children for permanence. Permanence must ensure that children's needs are met in the immediate and the long term and that they are held in their parent's mind into adulthood. This task requires a multi-disciplinary and multi-layered approach which supports the child, their foster family and their receiving family. The network of adults involved in planning permanency for children become connected in a complex web of procedures and decision-making, and sadly, the knowledge of the child and his experiences – the lived experience of being with them and knowing all that they are – can be lost. A child's experience on paper is only a part of their story. As Winnicott (1984) says, 'In every child there is a story that needs to be told – a story that no one else has yet had time to listen to'.

What are the tasks in preparing a child for permanence?

The social worker working with a child can act as a catalyst for change. The child who can respond positively to their social worker develops greater self-esteem while learning new and positive behaviour, which can then be transferred to their adoptive family. So preparing a child for this significant move is a critical process. The

importance of meeting the child's basic needs for security and routine is apparent, but other tasks include the following.

- **Enabling the child to experience and be aware of dependence on an adult.** Children with a disturbed sense of trust can have difficulty accepting their own needs for affection and closeness.

- **Helping the child to become more alert to people and events in the outside world by using all the senses.** Children in a constant state of tension can have distorted perceptions of the world and mistrust the information from their own senses.

- **Helping the child to identify and express feelings through creative play.** Children and young people can be confused and frightened by their emotions, especially simultaneous contradictory feelings such as anger and sadness.

- **Helping the child to clarify his life history.** Children and young people in care often have an uncertain sense of continuity and identity and life story work, when undertaken in a timely and thoughtful way, can help the child make sense of the past and who they are.

- **Helping the child to move on to new family relationships with the help of people from the past.** Children benefit from the permission of a family member to become adopted into a new family or be a permanent member of a foster family.

- **Helping the child to have fun.** Positive experiences build self-confidence, self-esteem and resilience, which separated and abused children often lack.

- **Helping the child to decide if he really wants an adoptive family.** Many children experience conflicting loyalties and making realistic choices for the future can feel desperately painful and laden with guilt.

Working closely with children experiencing such powerful emotions can be risky for workers too. Workers are often challenged by delay, lack of resources, poor support and too many children to think about. The ability to make objective decisions regarding permanency under these conditions can be compromised. The task for the network, and particularly for foster carers and social workers, is to help the child to understand why they are here and to help them make new permanent connections with the least delay.

The role of the worker in preparing parents for adoption

Adoption is a life-long commitment, and prospective parents benefit from careful preparation. To prepare prospective adopters to receive a child into their family, social workers need to provide:

- education about adoption and the care journey in its complexities;

- knowledge of normal child development;

- an understanding of the strategies that a child may use to regulate the proximity between themselves and their primary carer;

- an understanding about how to facilitate play experiences which will help the child to relax and develop a sense of trust in himself, his carer and eventually in others;

- a safe base which provides the containment for children to experience and work through their experiences of separation from and loss of their birth parents – even if their parents were abusive or lacking in parental capacity;

- a narrative of the child's life prepared with confidence and empathy, which is integrated into the child's understanding of their place in the world.

Acquiring this knowledge and understanding about the child's history and needs, combined with learnt skills about how to create a safe and nurturing environment in which the child can develop and grow, will help adoptive families feel empowered to take on full parenting responsibilities.

2 Assessing children for permanence

If the wishes and feelings of a child are to be sought in a meaningful way and he is to be helped to understand over time what adoption or permanence will mean for him now and in the longer term, careful and thorough work in an attuned relationship with the child is necessary (Luckock and Lefevre, 2008). Skills in communicating with him in a way that is accessible and meaningful and in which he can also make his thoughts, fears and feelings known can lead to a better understanding of the child. It is important to reassure the child that he is not being asked to bear the weight of the decision that needs to be made about permanence, but that his views are valued. His wishes and fears can be explored within a play environment through engagement, observation and reflection of what is observed and shared with the worker or carer. Communication with the child is important to inform the assessment and ensure that the child's wishes are ascertained. This in itself is of therapeutic value to the child, who can feel he has some involvement in what can be a confused and chaotic time and that he is central to the process.

The assessment report

The child's permanence report (CPR) is an important document in planning for the child's future and developing an adoption preparation plan. It is really important that the child's social worker learns as much as possible about the child's experiences, including the nature of care in the birth family, and the losses, separations and attachments, both in the birth family and in foster care. This information can inform an understanding of the child's internal working model and the strategies the child has learned to keep himself safe – his attachment strategy.

The form used to record the assessment of the child has been designed in accordance with statutory requirements and is therefore slightly different in different parts of the UK. However, there is more that is similar than not, as the purpose of a good assessment is to gain the best information about the child's history, and thereby an understanding of the child's needs. In England and Wales, it is required that a Child's Permanence Report (England: Form CPR) or a Child's Adoption Assessment Report (Wales: Form CAAR) are used; in Scotland and Ireland, the assessment is compiled on Form E. (These forms are produced and available from BAAF.)

The information gathered during the assessment can assist this process because it brings together important information, including:

● information about the child and his birth family;

● a summary by the medical adviser of the child's health;

● the wishes and feelings of the child, which have been carefully explored;

● the child's religious and cultural upbringing;

● contact arrangements or recommendations;

● the agency's view about contact needs and arrangements;

● the wishes and feelings of the birth parent/guardian;

● an assessment of the child's emotional and behavioural development, and other needs;

● an assessment of the parenting capacity of the child's parent/guardian;

● a chronology of decisions and actions taken by the local authority;

- an analysis of options for future care and why adoption is considered the preferred option;

- any other relevant information.

The importance of a chronology of events cannot be overestimated. The chronology helps a worker understand the child's life experience, and the exercise of compiling and gathering the information enables the worker to gain a real sense of the likely impact of that experience on the child. The synthesis of this information can aid an empathic understanding of the child's needs and more accurate planning, preparation and support for the receiving family.

As explained above, different forms are used in different parts of the UK to record the assessment on the child. It should also be noted that new adoption legislation has recently been passed in Scotland, and a new child assessment report will be needed in due course. In Northern Ireland, an adoption policy review is expected to lead to new adoption legislation, whereupon a new assessment form will need to be designed. Below, we look at the purpose of an assessment, but with reference to the Child's Permanence Report (CPR) (the Child's Adoption Assessment Report in Wales is very similar) for ease of reference and reading.

The CPR is a vital and lengthy document. Its purpose is to enable the adoption panel and agency decision-maker to discharge their functions under the Adoption Agencies Regulations, including compliance with the Welfare Checklist (s1 of the Adoption and Children Act 2002 (ACA 2002)), and to decide:

- whether to recommend that the child should be placed for adoption;

- whether to recommend that the child should be placed with prospective adopters;

and to provide:

- a source of information to be given to prospective adopters, which will enable them to decide whether or not to proceed with the matching process;

- a source of information about the child's background and heritage for adopters, once the child is placed;

- a record for the adopted adult of important information and detail about their life history and heritage;

- a referral form for the Adoption Register for England and Wales (if the Adoption Register is to be used to find a family).

The CPR is undertaken by a social worker who will collate and analyse birth family information, and placement, developmental, medical, educational, psychological and psychiatric histories and/or assessments that have been undertaken throughout the care process. The social worker also seeks information from individuals other than immediate family members, who are important to the child and who may be available to help the child move on. The child may be able to contribute to this too if the worker is involved in direct work with him, and sensitive communication skills are needed for this. Complete and accurate material from the case record is essential for the life story process and for preparing parents about the needs of the child.

The preparation of the CPR and involvement of the birth family in collecting and making sense of the information is a skilled and delicate task. Birth parents have the right to see information about them and their child presented to panel and they also have a right to see the finished document.

Long delays in planning for children are no longer acceptable, and the Adoption and Children Act 2002 (ACA 2002), through the welfare checklist, ensures that, when a decision relating to adoption is made, the welfare of the child must be the paramount consideration. The welfare checklist aims to avoid delay in coming to a decision as this is likely to impede or prejudice the child's welfare and well-being and make transitions increasingly difficult.

The welfare checklist requires that consideration be given to the social, emotional, cultural, religious and linguistic needs and wishes of the child. The social worker must assess the relationship with relatives and other relevant people connected with the child, and consider the likelihood of this relationship continuing and the ability of this person to provide a secure environment. It is important for the social worker to assess their wishes and feelings regarding the child.

Interviewing adults who know the child well

Social workers seek multiple perspectives on each child's behaviour, history and relationships by interviewing birth family members, foster carers, children's home workers, teachers, therapists, social workers, etc. These adults help fill in the gaps in the case record and clarify life history, especially details about past placements, and help paint a multifaceted picture of the child. Social workers ask those who know the child well to provide factual information on such characteristics as the child's sense of values, co-operation, style of play, sexuality, self-direction and self-control. To fully understand the child, it is also important to take account of the child's heritage and culture and the family rituals and traditions which inform his values and beliefs. These can often be seen when observing the child at play. Sensitivity to cultural issues in children's play is important as this can help the child to feel accepted and valued. To become competent in working with diversity requires openness, knowledge and reflection, and the capacity to be humble but curious in the face of not knowing. (For a rich source of multicultural play resources, see Gil and Drewes, 2006.)

Like all of us, children have many parts. They can be happy, angry, grumpy, excited, sad, bored… and the part that is shown is often a response to the child's social and emotional environment and indicative of the strategies he has developed within that context. When working with children who have been harmed or traumatised, it is sometimes difficult to see past that part of them. In gathering information for an assessment, it is really important to hold onto an idea that there is more to the child than their abuse.

Information gathered during assessment is particularly relevant because these early records give core information about the child's birth family, their environment and how these impacted on the child's development and well-being. Understanding the intricate dynamics of environment, parenting capacity and its effect on the child's development can give clues about the internal working model the child may have developed. As the relationship between worker and child develops, the worker's knowledge of child development and attachment theory informs an understanding and an analysis of the strategies that the child has hitherto developed to manage his environment and relationships. Such knowledge and analysis will assist the decision making about matching and any therapeutic support the child may need.

Meeting the child

The social worker will want to interact with the child, and indeed may have known the child from the very earliest referral to the social services department. This interaction is an important part of the evaluation process, as the child is likely to demonstrate those behaviours that he or she will show other adults, including future carers. In the assessment, workers include: a physical description of the child; a description of the child's way of making contact with others; a description of his level of animation, sense of humour, curiosity, confidence and sense of self; his cognitive abilities, coping styles, and openness to change his culture and family experience. Workers then evaluate the impact of each of these considerations on the prospective parents. This can help the worker and parent anticipate some of the child's future interactions with other adults.

Knowledge of child development milestones

A flow chart can be used to represent graphically the child's placement history and the child can be involved in constructing this. An accurate chronology on the file will help too. This facilitates a comparison between the child's experience and expected child development. It helps to target developmental milestones, such as those described by Erikson (or Gesell), which may have been adversely affected by untimely separations, neglect and abuse. Many children in the looked after system need help to address gaps in development and emotional or mental health issues. It may be necessary to seek specific support for the child such as play therapy or filial therapy or other parent–child support programmes, and this is explored in later chapters.

Determining the child's view of family, permanence and the future

In meetings with the child, the worker needs to seek information regarding the child's feelings about significant figures in his life, his understanding of his experiences so far and the child's knowledge of his past history. The worker needs to know whether the child feels he belongs somewhere other than his present residence, or if residential care staff or the foster family is the only family known to the child. The worker also needs to ascertain the child's vision of his future: Does he envisage a reunion with his birth parents or other birth family members? Or does the child imagine being with a new family? (Chapter 3 describes techniques for gathering this information and a discussion of first meetings.)

Making a preparation plan

During the assessment process, it may become apparent that the child has very specific needs and that a more specialist assessment is required. Such assessments are now undertaken by multi-professional teams; this, in turn, informs a relevant and meaningful plan for the child.

The assessment helps the worker determine which aspects of preparation should be stressed. For example, sensory development work may be a priority for a child with severe early deprivation. For a child whose sense of autonomy and dependence is imbalanced, facilitating appropriate dependence may be helpful. Expressing grief and other feelings through creative play is encouraged for children whose anger or sadness needs a constructive outlet. Life story work (Ryan and Walker, 2007) is important for all children in foster care, and help to say goodbye to birth family members is necessary for children who require permission from an important adult to make new family ties. If a child's adoption preparation needs are beyond current abilities and resources, staff must make recommendations for alternative services. The Adoption and Children Act 2002 requires local authorities in England and Wales to provide information about the adoption service as well as information and support services during and after adoption for children, birth families and adopters. Local authorities also have a duty to assess the needs of individuals requesting services. In Scotland, the Adoption and Children (Scotland) Act 2005 has a similar requirement. In Northern Ireland, local authorities have a duty to provide post-placement support to adoptive parents.

For the child, the continuing assessment and preparation process opens up opportunities to help the child develop a more positive self-image, enhanced interpersonal skills, and a view of the past and the future from a position of greater strength and resilience. Continuing direct work (Luckock and Lefevre, 2008) with the child can also help to introduce the child to the concept of adoption, and to different family structures (a picture book for young children published by BAAF (Griffiths, 2007) can help with this task). For the future adoptive parent or carer, the process provides a more complete picture of the child and will alert them to the child's behaviour and what to expect once the child is placed with them. This understanding will have been enhanced in adoption preparation groups. However, as Janet, an adoptive mother, said, she could never be prepared for the maelstrom which hit her life in the shape of two-and-a-half-year-old Ellie:

> I thought I was a coping and competent woman. For years I have held a challenging job working with difficult people. We had waited a long time for our daughter and although we had been told about "issues", to be honest we had really thought, how hard can it be – she's only a baby!

Such feelings are echoed by many. Although adopter preparation groups can alert prospective adopters to the types of children needing adoptive families, their characteristics and likely histories, they understandably fall short of preparing adoptive families for the specific child or children whom they are likely to parent. Foster carers take many children into their homes over time and experience this maelstrom repeatedly.

The assessment process must take into account the social, cognitive and emotional level of the child; the child's confidence in those around him; the child's desire or ability to engage in specific types of creative techniques; the child's level of ambivalence regarding adoption; and the child's knowledge and acceptance of his life history.

Information can be gained about a child from reading the case record but this should be informed by interviewing others and spending time with the child. Workers should not be discouraged if they feel they are just getting to know a child after several meetings. Both the assessment and the preparation processes are ongoing.

It is apparent that the need to engage with the child early, and in a consistent way, is necessary to achieve good outcomes. Children do not work to timescales, so planning for ongoing support and containment of confusion, distress and grief are essential.

3 Some ways to begin

If, after the core assessment has been completed and a plan put in place to support the child and birth family, it becomes apparent that the parenting capacity and the environmental factors are not conducive to returning the child to their birth family (Department of Health, 2004), the social worker will be aware that there is a long journey ahead which may involve conflict, litigation, movement and change for the child. At this early stage, it is not known what the outcome for the child and family will be and often planning is like juggling balls in the air, with a round of assessments, reports, contact visits, appointments and new or changing professionals moving in and out of the scene.

Where is the child in this?

Children react in many ways to being removed from their birth family, including relief, compliance, confusion, sadness or rage – or a mix of all of these. A new social worker, alternative foster carer or support worker might meet the child at any point in these times of uncertainty and transition. As the child's social worker, you may have known her since the case came into the duty and assessment team or transferred to the long-term team. There is an important role for you, as a consistent person in the child's life, to link up her past history with her present. And if, as many social workers do, you remain allocated to the child until permanent placement, there are many opportunities to engage with her and help her begin to process her experiences. This is not easy if she is angry, dismissive or ambivalent towards you. It is helpful to hold on to the idea that the strategies the child employs with you to control her closeness or distance from you are those which have served to keep her safe in the past.

Remember, in your early sessions with the child you will want to:

- get to know each other and establish your boundaries for working together, establish a rapport and be alert to the modes of expression that are most comfortable for the child, i.e. visual, tactile, verbal, play;

- begin to gather information for assessment including information about the child's connections with others, her view of the future and the possibility of an alternative family, and her construction of her life history.

Introductions

The worker's job is to help plan for the child's future, and this role should be described to the child so that she is clear about who you are and what you do. First meetings are critical and it can help to liaise with the foster carer or other workers in advance to discuss how they can introduce you and your role. Children often appreciate a letter or card in advance explaining who you are and why you are visiting them. You could even scan in your picture.

It can help to meet the child in their most secure place and with their carer or social worker. If your intention is to use the time in play with the child, it is helpful to have some toys or activities with you to offer.

Building rapport between worker and child

Building rapport is about developing a way of communicating which reflects or has resonance with the person you are in dialogue with. The aim for the adults in the network around the child is to develop a relationship in which a child can collaborate in the tasks related to the preparation for moving on or permanence. Within the relationship, the child needs the opportunity to express her feelings and process her history. Social workers need to create relationships in which children can feel accepted and important – establishing regular visiting schedules and routines attached to visits will enhance the child's sense of safety and sense of trust.

If adults are attuned to children, they soon learn the rhythms and patterns of the child's communication. Some children are comfortable with exploring their feelings through drawing or writing stories; some act out their feelings with toys; others want to communicate their experiences verbally. It is helpful to have a variety of materials available, such as toys, books, crayons, games or clay (see Auerbach, 1999, for some suggestions). Realistically, a busy social worker will not have the resources available to allow the optimum choice for the child and may need to find other creative ways of working with her. It is perhaps useful here to distinguish between play therapy and direct work.

Play therapy

The role of the social worker has changed significantly in recent years; increasingly, they are case managers and co-ordinators and the time which they can spend in dialogue with children is continually eroded. Children received into care present complex problems and it is increasingly the case that the work of processing the past and integrating the preparation for their future permanence is undertaken by specialist CAMHS workers, or commissioned out to specialist social workers.

Play therapy is becoming an increasingly preferred option to assist children to process traumatic experiences. There are various models of play therapy (see Chapter 7), but the method of choice is usually determined by the availability of a therapist and the resources to fund them. Play therapy *is* therapy and should be undertaken as a relatively long-term commitment with a trained and skilled therapist who has an understanding of the very particular issues of abuse, trauma and disrupted attachment that children bring to their placements. Not all children have access to or need this intervention. But there are ways to use therapeutic play skills to build relationships with children and thereby enable their participation in the planning process. Spaulding social workers suggest appealing at a sensory level with the use of mood music, such as ocean sounds, which can help to create a relaxing atmosphere, or by sharing food or other sensory experiences. Lack of working space might determine that a busy social worker will enjoy the opportunity to take the child out to the park or to a café as an ice-breaker, but this should not become the predictable routine that the child expects.

Sharing food: Melvin

Melvin, aged five, was living with a foster family who were uncertain about adopting him because of his learning disabilities. On the first visit to the foster family, the worker brought a box of animal crackers and encouraged Melvin to look at the box and name each animal on it. At first Melvin only wanted to eat, but eventually he slowed down and identified each animal. He repeatedly ran to his foster mother to show her the animal crackers.

The worker brought out paper and crayons and encouraged Melvin to draw one of the animals. He chose an elephant and became intensely involved in his work, drawing violent scribbles off the page. The story he told about the picture was: 'Once upon a time, there was a little big elephant. And a little star went in the cage. And then the little star flew in the track.' Later, Melvin and his worker cut out an elephant from the box of crackers. Melvin treasured the cut-out and showed it to his foster carer when he came home.

This session created a relaxed, productive atmosphere and set the tone for further work together. The exercise enabled the worker to see how Melvin approached problems. His artwork,

PHOTO © HELEN JOUBERT

which amounted to scribbles, with no recognisable figure and story, seemed more appropriate for a child of three or four than a five-year-old. The session also showed how free Melvin was to engage in creative play, how he interacted with his foster carers, and how they interacted with him. Melvin's easy transition from eating crackers to intense drawing, storytelling, and sharing of his work with others suggested that he could progress to other creative preparation techniques regarding moving to an adoptive family ●

It is more productive for the worker to proceed at the child's pace in a spirit of acceptance than to rush the child for the purposes of deadlines. This is always a dilemma. The example above illustrates the importance of sharing in the child's interests and – much like the story of the tortoise and the hare – slow and steady wins the race.

 ## Connecting though the senses of taste and smell: Tom

Tom, a 12-year-old boy, appeared very depressed and withdrawn. When the worker first met Tom, he lived in a home for children with developmental disabilities. Each time his worker came to visit Tom, she brought fruit or nuts – oranges, peaches, raisins, walnuts. Although Tom often appeared tense and silent with adults, he was happy to share the food with his worker and looked forward to the snack as a kind of ritual the two shared. Tom felt comfortable talking about the food and enjoyed the juicy mess they made together.

Engagement in a shared activity provides a sense of connection and safety which encourages children to explore their experiences. With Tom, who was withdrawn and unable to think meaningfully about adoption in these early stages, the sharing of fruit led to preliminary preparation work aimed at reducing his depression. (Further work with Tom is described in Chapter 4 on experiencing through the senses.)

Using the senses of touch and smell: Diane

Meeting Diane, aged 12, the worker found a constricted little girl, arms held tightly to her sides. As the worker spoke, Diane looked straight in front of her. She gave brief, expressionless responses to questions about the children's home where she lived. Finally Diane announced: 'Nobody likes me, and I don't like anybody.' The worker noticed that Diane's fingernails were bitten and sore and her hands looked painfully dry. The worker had some scented hand cream with her, which she offered to Diane.

Worker: *I have something you might like. It's hand cream. Can I rub some on your hands? (Diane quietly accepts.) Doesn't that feel good? You know this smells nice too. Can you smell it? What does it smell like?*

Diane: *I don't know.*

Worker: *Smells like roses. Did you ever smell a rose?*

Diane: *No.*

Worker: *What's your favourite flower? (Diane shrugs.) I'll bring you a rose next time and we can smell it.*

In this example, the worker began to model the continuity and trust which Diane will later come to expect in a parenting figure. The nurturing process created an atmosphere of acceptance. Diane felt very important when she received a rose on the next visit. Diane was slow to become more actively engaged in the preparation process. Her feelings of worthlessness and her experiences of early deprivation signalled the need for preparation work using nurturing exercises. (See Chapter 4 for further work with Diane.)

Connecting through touch: Jen

Jen was 15 and, following a series of placement breakdowns because of her violence and absconding, had been placed in a secure unit. She was verbally aggressive and resistant to any worker's involvement.

Her CAMHS worker made a series of appointments and wrote them down for her. Jen refused to attend and consistently ignored the worker who turned up regularly and each time left a note for her until, after a number of sessions, Jen agreed to see her and told her about her interest in being a nail technician. She asked the worker if she could do her nails and the worker agreed for next time. On arrival, Jen had set out her nail polishes, remover, cotton wool, and a bowl of warm water, soap and a towel. She carefully and tenderly washed her worker's hands and dried them and painted her nails. All the time she talked about her worry for her mother, who was a substance abuser, and how she wished she could do this for her.

From that point, Jen was able to engage in the work and a supportive relationship developed, which remained important to Jen for a considerable time ●

When working with children, touch presents difficult dilemmas. An emphasis on child protection and safeguarding has encouraged "no touch" policies in most agencies, and where touch is seen to be appropriate in an intervention, this should be discussed and anchored in supervision. Ideally, the child's carer or parent should be involved.

What is happening in these scenarios?

In the first two case studies, the worker is approaching the child in a direct way with small treats. Initially, the engagement for the child is the treat, but as the worker becomes predictable and undemanding, the child is able to relax into the relationship. In the third scenario, the worker hears the subtext of Jen's request – do you trust me to do this? – and accepts Jen's need to test her.

Clearly, the situations given above will be mediated by gender, age and ability, but there are some keys to good communication demonstrated here which can provide the cornerstones to building relationships through play, creative activity or dialogue. These principles were first promoted by Virginia Axline (1947, p73–74), who suggested that, to be with children in a therapeutic way, it is necessary to:

- develop a warm and friendly relationship with the child;

- accept the child as she or he is;

- establish a feeling of permission in the relationship so that the child feels free to express his or her feelings completely;

- remain alert to recognise the feelings the child is expressing and reflect these feelings back in such a manner that the child gains insight into his/her behaviour;

- maintain a deep respect for the child's ability to solve his/her problems and give the child the opportunity to do so – the responsibility to make choices and to institute change is the child's;

- not attempt to direct the child's actions or conversations in any manner – the child leads the way, the therapist follows;

- not hurry the therapy along – it is a gradual process and must be recognised as such by the therapist;

- only establish those limitations necessary to anchor the therapy to the world of reality and to make the child aware of his/her responsibility in the relationship.

Establishing a relationship on the basis of these principles need not take a long time and does not demand expensive resources – it is about being with the child in such a way that the arousal–relaxation cycle is consistently rehearsed. A relationship is most likely to develop with children by being with them in play rather than through interview.

However, making interventions such as these may feel uncomfortable for a busy worker who is encouraged to case-manage rather than casework. It helps to have discussed with a supervisor and with the child's foster carer the way in which you are going to work. From the child's perspective, it might feel strange to experience an adult's genuine interest in her and she might be wary, being more used to being questioned by adults than having them attend to her.

Identifying significant others

Even when children have been separated from families who have harmed them, it is important to remember that birth family members are highly significant in children's lives and there may be others – previous social workers, carers, teachers and neighbours – who have been important in the child's development. There may also be unknown significant others about whom the child feels ambivalence, fear or dislike. A technique suggested by Spaulding to collect this information is the "holiday trip", in which the child is asked to imagine a holiday anywhere in the world and name anyone she wants to bring along.

 ### The holiday trip: Janie

Janie, aged 11, was living in a children's home.

Worker: *We're going to play an imagination game. Let's pretend that you could go on a holiday anywhere at all. Anywhere in the world. Where would you go?*

Janie: *To Disney World.*

Worker: *Let's say you could have two holiday homes at Disney World: one for yourself and anyone else you wanted, and another one for other people you wanted to bring along. (Draws two houses.) Who would be in this first one?*

Janie: *Me and Dawn and Chantelle.*

Worker: *And in the second?*

Janie: *Tiffany, Lisa and Lesley.*

The worker established that the people named were all other girls in the children's home where Janie lived. The worker checked whether Janie would take any adults along, and she named a woman who was a member of staff at the home. Janie named nobody from her past life. Perhaps she was being realistic about the actual cut-off from parents who had abandoned her. Perhaps she was just not willing to speak about them. In either case, the worker needed to learn more about Janie's connections with people from her past, but in the meantime, she had identified an adult who was important to Janie and who could be helpful in supporting her through the pre-placement process.

The worker's next step was to learn more from the staff at the children's home. She discovered that Janie had been separated from alcoholic parents only a year earlier. She was mourning silently. She would avoid talking about her old family life, except to defend her parents occasionally.

With this background information, the worker could make a plan, working at Janie's pace, in coming to grips with painful family facts. Using play materials over a series of meetings, Janie had a chance to "tell" her story to herself and to the worker. (See Chapter 5 for more about the preparation process with Janie.)

The holiday trip: Robert

Robert, a 13-year-old who had previously spent many years in a children's home, had just experienced a disruption from a single-parent adoptive family. His new worker engaged Robert in the holiday trip game. Robert listed his adoptive father and the father's friends and relatives in one vacation house.

Robert had vivid fantasies of returning to this family. It was clear that the family had to deliver a stronger message to the child that this was not possible. The father wrote a letter to Robert stating how much he cared for him, but how he knew they could never be reunited.

The holiday trip: Steven and Jamie

Steven, a ten-year-old who also lived in a children's home, wanted to bring his volunteer "big brother" on his holiday trip. This process led to a discussion of Steven's dream of being adopted by his "big brother", and some necessary clarification work ensued.

Jamie, aged eight, said that he would take along his birth parents, giving their full names. Staff had believed that Jamie remembered nothing about his birth family. The holiday trip provided a way to discuss this "secret" information with him.

The child's view of the future and adoption

Some children say directly that they do or do not want to be adopted, or that they want to return to their birth mother, or that they want to go to a group home. With adolescents who are uncertain about future permanence, workers use an exercise called "future paths" which emphasises that it is the child's decision to choose adoption or independent living. The worker then focuses on developing future goals with the young person.

Future paths: Alice

Alice, aged 13, had experienced many placements and generally avoided talking about permanence. This is an early discussion with her worker.

Worker: *You know, Alice, we haven't really talked about your future. Let's look today at the choices you might have. We'll call this Alice's Future Paths. (Writes this across the top of a blank sheet of paper.)*

Alice: *What's "paths"?*

Worker: *Those are the different ways a person can go in the years ahead. Let's say this is the road you came on. (Quickly sketches in houses.) You lived with your grandma, then in a foster home, then (names foster placements) and now you're here. Where could you go from here? (Draws some branching paths.) What's this first one?*

Alice: *The first is up to heaven. (Takes crayon and draws an arrow pointing upward.)*

Worker: *(Surprised, a bit alarmed.) So that's the first one. Why up to heaven?*

Alice: *Because it's peaceful there. Here there's nothing but fighting. Kids fighting with me all the time.*

Worker: *Any other choices? Where do these other paths go?*

(Alice writes "Being a singer or lawyer" and "Going to my real parents".)

Worker: *There's one path left. Could that be the path to an adoption home?*

Alice: *I don't want to be adopted.*

Worker: *Well, what about your other paths? The first one, up to heaven, where it's peaceful. Did someone tell you once that that's the place to be?*

Alice: *My grandma always used to say that. There's no peace on earth, only in heaven. (Pauses.) And I could see her there.*

Worker: *I can see that you don't want to think about an adoption home. You still think about being with your grandma. And maybe you also think about some of the foster parents you cared about.*

Alice: *But I do want a family. (Writes "adoption family" on the last path.)*

Worker: *It sounds like you feel partly "yes" and partly "no" about a new family.*

Alice: *Yeah…It's hard for me. It's partly "yes" and partly "no". (Writes this on the chart.) I really had a lot of families. How many did I have? I think I had 36.*

Worker: *I'll be checking your old records this week, so next time I can tell you how many. And you can tell me what you remember.*

After this exchange, the worker let staff at the children's home know about the depressed, hopeless note Alice sounded here. She also enquired about the fighting that bothered Alice so much, indicative of the stresses in the residential unit with which Alice was not coping well. Alice seemed ready to start her life story book (more about the life story process in Chapter 6) and, in future sessions, the worker started talking with Alice about her foster families and her memories of her grandmother.

Future paths: Ellie

Ellie, 11 years old, was living with a foster family who had requested her removal.

Worker: *Let's talk about your wishes for the future. Let's look at the paths you might take in the years to come. (Worker draws several paths from the present foster home.) What do you wish for your paths to the future?*

Ellie: *I wish I got a nice family and I finish school. (Ellie writes this on the first path.) I wish my brother and my mother will be OK.*

Worker: *It sounds like you worry about them.*

Ellie: *Sometimes, because my mother drinks too much and she doesn't take care of my little sister. My brother yells at her and tells her he's going to call the police.*

Worker: *You wish they will be OK and you wish you had a nice family for yourself. Tell me about these other wishes for your future.*

Ellie: *I want to be a model. I want a big car and lots of money.*

Worker: *There's another path left. (Ellie writes "marriage".)*

Ellie's dream of a "good" family showed recognition that her birth and foster families were not helpful aspirations for her. Ellie appeared disposed towards being placed with a new family, though her ambivalence towards her mother – her worry about her and anger towards her – could interfere with her attachment to a new family, indicating that further work might help her to resolve her anxiety about her siblings – and indeed about her mother – and feel less guilt about moving forward. The information gained from this exercise may contribute to a decision about contact now and in the future. If it were possible to also work with Ellie's mother to ensure that the contact is fruitful for them, Ellie may be supported into future permanence.

The child's vision for her future – the "miracle question"

When preparing a child for placement, it is important to work out the child's narrative of her preferred future life. Over time the narrative can be developed, added to and clarified as the worker and child explore possibilities. A helpful way of developing the narrative is to use the "miracle question" (developed by Miller and Berg, and discussed in Stringer and Mall (1999, p 109)):

- Imagine that after you have gone to bed tonight a miracle happens and your life is as you want it to be – but because you were asleep, you will not know that the miracle has happened. When you wake up tomorrow morning, what will be different that will tell you a miracle has happened? What else…? What else…?

Setting the scene in this way is important and if you are curious and interested, and possibly even excited by the possibilities, this might transfer to the young person. You can continue with the following possibilities, remembering to keep the discussion light and playful. The child can draw her possibilities if she wishes or paint or collage them.

- What will you be doing differently? What else…?

- Who will be there to notice?

- How will your mum/dad/teacher/other know that the miracle has happened?

- What will others notice you doing differently?

- In this future time when life is as you want it and you are living in a family/on your own/with a mum/dad/your siblings/in a home, how will you know that life is going well for you?

These questions will elicit hopes and fears and begin to develop possibilities for a preferred future.

- What will tell you that you don't need to come here any more or that this future place is right for you?

- Imagine a day going well – how will you know the day is going well?

- Imagine this new family turns out to be more useful than you thought it would: how will you know? What will be different in your life?

- How will you know that this placement has been useful to you?

- Imagine that you take back control of your life and you are feeling that this is the life/ family/situation that you want – how will you know that you are living a life that is right for you?

The emphasis is on the possibilities of life being as the child hopes in the future – *the child's vision*.

Hopes for the future: David

Worker: *David, I'm going to be reading your case files – about your family and about the places you've lived. I need to know about your past to help plan for your future. Is there anything you want me to try to find out when I read the record? Anything about when you were younger, or about your family, or the other places you've lived?*

David: *I want to know where my brothers and sisters are.*

Worker: *I can find out. Anything else?*

David: *I want to know where my mother is. And I want to know how many places I lived. Somebody told me 15.*

It is clear from this exchange that David's vision of his past was a muddle. He was interested in knowing something about his past moves and about the present circumstances of his family members. When it came time to start the life story work, David was curious because he had already formulated questions for which the worker then had some answers ●

A life journey chart provides information about the child's knowledge of his or her history, and lets the worker know whether the child is open to talking about the past. The life journey chart is actually a flow chart constructed by the child of all the places in which he or she has lived. It often paves the way for future life story work.

Life journey chart: Robert

Robert's life journey chart was begun following a disruption from an adoptive placement. His new worker introduced the chart on her first visit.

Worker: *I need to get to know you better since I'm going to be your new social worker. I don't know very much about you and your life history yet, so I'd like you to tell me what you know about it. We can make a picture of your history on this page. Here's where you were born. (Draws a hospital.) Let's write your birth date. What is it?*

Robert: *April 10th.*

Worker: *(Draws another building.) Where were you born and whom did you live with?*

Robert: *Glasgow. That lady…Joanne.*

The worker established that Joanne was his birth mother. This brief exchange suggested that Robert had strong, angry feelings towards his birth mother – notice that he names her as 'that lady' – and that he wanted to give the impression that he did not claim her as his mother.

Robert knew much of his placement history, but this process helped him and his worker raise specific questions about his life and the families he had lived with. The worker agreed to seek these answers in the next few weeks as she read Robert's case records ●

Children can have a multitude of feelings towards their birth family, ranging from loss and grief through to anger and ambivalence. Whatever their feelings, they will be mixed with confusion about what has happened, uncertainty about their own part in the experience and confusion and anxiety about the future. Working with children experiencing these feelings takes time and a genuine interest and concern for the child. Children have uncanny antennae to know when the adult interacting with them – whether that is a social worker, residential worker, foster carer or school teacher – is genuinely interested in them.

4 Renurturing techniques

Play and its nurturing components

Once the child's assessment has been completed, the preparation for permanence proceeds, based on the needs of the child. Children who have been harmed will be wary and cautious with adults and may not respond to traditional interviewing techniques, direct work sheets or treats and occasional activities. Many do respond to play and will play in the presence of an adult who is non-intrusive, respectful, accepting and, most of all, curious. In this context, this means that the worker has a real wish to understand the meaning of the behaviour or the play sequence that is before them. Children often engage in play with an overt nurturing component. Workers can use:

- sensory development techniques to promote learning through the senses and to help children become more open to the world and their own experiences;

- early nurture exercises on the needs of babies to help children recognise that they both require and deserve good parenting;

- Storytelling, which can provide an opportunity for closeness and warmth;

- continuity work, which includes using special places and rituals to emphasise constancy and continuity for the child;

- the "lost object": a special toy which symbolically replaces some of the experiences the child has missed or lost;

- relaxation, which helps the child calm down and have positive experiences with rules, boundaries and self-control.

The worker, in his or her regular meetings with the child, can help when he is seemingly "stuck"

at the emotional level at which his trauma occurred. Attending to and tracking the play and naming the feelings which seem to be present can help to develop the child's trust in the adult and develop more positive and appropriate attachment behaviour (this is explored more fully in Chapter 7). Read the following dialogue between a child and her carer. Notice:

- how carefully the carer attends to and tracks play;

- how she lets Amy take the lead;

- how she accepts Amy's choices.

Testing for safety and protection: Amy

Amy is exploring the toys in the toy box.

Amy: *What's this?*

Carer: *It's whatever you want it to be.*

Amy: *Is it a monster?*

Carer: *It made you think of a monster.*

Amy: *It's dangerous.*

Carer: *You think it's dangerous and there might be some dangerous things in there.*

Amy: *Y.e.e.e.s.s.*

Carer: *It's a worry if you think that maybe you are not safe enough in here...*

Amy: *(finds a shiny frog) I saw this at my house – it made me sick but this doesn't.*

Carer: *You felt sick at home but not here.*

Looking after frog

Amy finds a square of shiny fabric which she uses to wrap up the frog to keep him warm.

Amy: *This could be a cover for him.*

Carer: *A cover for him…you know just what he needs.*

Amy: *I will make him warm…*

Carer: *You can do that for him.*

Keeping tidy

Amy has sorted out from the toy box the toys she wants to use.

Amy: *I think we'll put those in here (in the play box). Yes?*

Carer: *You want those in the box and…*

Amy: *… Only keep ouuuutttt…(choosing toys to leave out)*

Carer: *You are choosing those…*

Amy: *I want to have out….(choosing toys and putting the others carefully away).*

Carer: *You are sorting things out.*

What is happening in this example? Firstly, Amy tested for safety and protection by querying if the toy she picked up is a monster. Her carer, commenting on the play, acknowledges how worrying it is to be unsure about being safe and Amy, perhaps stimulated by those feelings of anxiety, talks about home. The play then moves to a nurturing theme as Amy takes care of the frog and, without offering praise or compliments, the carer comments that Amy knows just what frogs need. To offer praise or a compliment might encourage Amy to repeat this sequence of play to please her carer or gain reward and could lay down a condition of worth, i.e. teach Amy that she has to behave in this way to please. This is not the aim – the aim is to have Amy explore what nurturing is. The carer's comment, 'You can do that for him….' helps Amy to experience some mastery. Amy appears to receive this implicit message because she moves to choosing, tidying and sorting. Again, the final comment, 'You are sorting things out', acknowledges that Amy can do this.

Read this play sequence again and consider:

● What has been experienced by the carer?

● What has been experienced by the child?

● What has been communicated between them?

Renurturing exercises can produce valuable information about the child's pattern of seeking closeness or using distancing behaviour, in other words, the attachment-eliciting or attachment-avoiding strategies that the child has developed to manage proximity with her carers. This information is invaluable to the adoptive parents receiving the child as they can be prepared for what can be overwhelming feelings of rejection when the child resists care or avoids approaching her new parents.

Sensory development techniques

Children who have experienced deprivation, neglect and abuse in their first years of life either have not been taught or choose not to use all their senses to understand the world. According to Cooper (1986) in her paper, *The Growing Child*, a young child needs to learn the different qualities of experiences, such as rough and smooth, acrid and sweet, melodic and cacophonous, or bright and muted, through educational experiences with others. The child who has not learned to make distinctions between sensory experiences is not only disadvantaged compared to other children, but is confused about herself, her body, and her environment. Life learning and experiencing happen in the context of a close and loving relationship with a safe primary carer who, in turn, stimulates and soothes the infant. This process leads to significant changes in the structure of the brain which provides the blueprint for future relationships and richness of future experiences. This blueprint is known as the internal working model – and we all have one.

Many looked after children will have been deprived of opportunities to learn through the senses. To help the child participate more actively in his or her experiences, parents and carers should encourage their child to identify sights, sounds, feelings, smells and tastes in a consistent but informal way. Sensory development can also be achieved through play and can help to create relationships based on trust which encourage attachment between the child and her parent. This work is especially useful for children whose social and emotional development is delayed, children who have been physically or sexually abused, and children who are depressed or withdrawn.

2009 © WENDY NERO. IMAGE FROM BIGSTOCKPHOTO.COM

Techniques designed to alert the senses not only help to engage children who are slow to participate in more advanced techniques, but also lay the foundations for enabling the child to better distinguish between the real world and her fantasy world. Some of these techniques lead to discussion of associations between specific experiences of tasting, touching and smelling and specific feelings. This work can lead the child to recall memories of other sensory experiences, both good and bad. For abused children, work around the sense of touch helps to distinguish among the many different kinds of touching. Some games used include "guess the fruit", to alert the senses of smell and taste, and the "feely bag", to develop the sense of touch.

The impact of trauma

Children experience danger and risk in many ways on a day-to-day basis – danger from roads, hot objects, bullies, etc, and most children will deal with fears by returning to a parent – a secure base – who will reassure and protect them. An experience of danger becomes traumatic when we perceive the threat to be life threatening or when we perceive a risk of serious injury; when this happens, we feel trapped and alone in the experience. Feelings of terror and helplessness can occur for children when the parent who should protect or rescue them is unavailable or is the source of the fear or danger. This is when experience becomes traumatic. These powerful, distressing emotions are accompanied by strong and frightening physical reactions, such as a rapid heartbeat, trembling, a feeling of the stomach dropping, and a sense of being in a dream.

Children come into the care system as a result of many factors coming together to cause them harm. The fact that they are in the care system means that something has gone terribly wrong in their lives and this always involves a breakdown of their closest relationships, either because their carers have done something to them – acts of commission – or failed to do something for them – acts of omission. Many of these experiences can be classified as "traumatic".

Some children may have experienced such episodes on an ongoing basis and display symptoms of post-traumatic stress as a result.

- Experiences remain imprinted on their minds and they may have repeated upsetting images or thoughts of past experiences – often when in relaxed states.

- Children may have disturbed sleep and nightmares and be stimulated to expressing strong physical and emotional reactions by seemingly innocuous events, which are reminders of past experiences.

- As a result it becomes difficult – sometimes even impossible – to distinguish new, safer situations or people from the traumatic situation already lived through.

- This leads to an avoidance of any situation, person or place that serves as a reminder of what happened, and the emotional energy expended in trying to keep the thoughts, feelings and images from returning distracts from learning and experience.

- Children may develop "amnesia", forgetting some of the worst parts of the experience, while continuing to react, often unconsciously, to reminders or triggers of the experience.

- It becomes imperative for the child to stay "on alert", causing difficulty in falling asleep (bedtimes can become highly fraught in families) or frequent waking, leading to irritability, tiredness and a lack of concentration.

- Some children may experience recurring physical symptoms, like headaches, stomach aches or feeling sick, and this can become a means of avoiding situations too.

Traumatic experiences impact emotionally, physically and cognitively too, as toxic levels of stress hormones (cortisol) pump around the body. Cortisol affects brain function, all major body systems and social functioning. It is secreted to enable the individual to respond to a threat (triggered by fear or uncertainty) and it acts to mobilise the body for a quick response to this threat, such as alertness, faster breathing and heart rate, and to minimise other body functions that are not essential to the immediate survival needs of the individual. Functions such as digestion, sexual behaviour, learning and rational thinking, amongst others, are shut down for the duration of the stress response. This is the case for even very young children who experience harm and the long-term effects can be devastating.

Children who have been physically harmed are often alert and vigilant to their environment and find it hard to settle into a flow of play. This vigilance underpinned by fear and anxiety needs to be named in the play for the child so that they become aware of their state of hyper-arousal. Play can help children revisit stressful experiences and "re-parent" themselves by, for example, engaging in doll and nurture play, or rescuing hurt pets so that the child can experience and explore the effects of nurturing behaviour – almost as if they are healing the hurt part of themselves, but in the presence of an attuned adult who can notice and validate this. Thus the child can learn to self-soothe.

Alerting the senses: Tom

Tom, a 12-year-old, had been removed from his mother's home some years earlier. In the disturbed home environment, he had developed a pattern of angry defiance, as well as messy and destructive behaviour. At the children's home, Tom craved attention from adults, but was often angry and oppositional. He was very negative about adoption at first. In the opening sessions, the worker approached Tom in a non-threatening way, using materials to alert the senses.

Worker: *Today we have some fruit, for a guessing game.*

Tom: *(From glum expression, to interest.) Where is it?*

Worker: *Close your eyes – and tell me what kind of fruit this smells like. (Tom closes eyes, worker holds out an orange.)*

Tom: *(Intent, inhaling.) That's an orange!*

The worker confirmed Tom's answer with enthusiasm and offered the orange for him to handle. She asked how the skin felt and Tom said: 'It's rough!' The worker and Tom tasted the orange and talked about its taste. Then they started "guessing" about an apple, examining and tasting that too. When they compared the fruit and talked about the different tastes, textures and colours, Tom commented that his favourite colour was red.

Sharing fruit became a ritual connecting Tom and the worker. Through this process, the worker communicated an acceptance of Tom and his need to move slowly regarding adoption. Tom mashed fruit, messed with it, played at being fed like a baby – and then gradually played at making up "recipes" and holding parties for himself and the worker. He also "messed" with lotions and shaving creams, mixing and touching and using them on himself. (This controlled, playful "messing" contrasted benignly with the hostile messing of his early years with his mother.)

This simple exercise led to a whole experience of being with an adult and enjoying other sensory experiences. The worker brought out some different coloured wools and a scrap-book. She suggested they begin Tom's life story book by putting his favourite colour wool in it. Tom became interested in cutting and pasting and composing a title for his book ●

If using this exercise, you could consider foods or fruits which may be culturally familiar to the child but not to you. Stimulating the senses to re-experience may also evoke conscious or unconscious memories. If the child is moved to anger, sadness, fear or other aroused states, the worker should remain curious about this and therefore not be overwhelmed by the child's response.

Tactile messy play can allow the child to regress and experience or re-experience a range of responses to the play material. Children can be attracted to or repulsed by messy play, depending on their lived experience. Tactile materials such as clay, dough and jelly can represent many things – children can manipulate it, destroy it, restore it and create with it. It can also be used to regress to babyhood as you smear it, touch and throw it – and even taste it. You can represent your own body as "sick" or "pooh" or other body fluids that are parts of yourself and re-experience all of those feelings that were not named for the child in their earliest days. However, when the child uses the play materials, they can re-experience and begin to overcome their trauma in a safe relationship. Play with messy tactile materials can also free the child to explore other sensory experiences, as Tom went on to do.

In another session, the worker played the "feely bag" guessing game. Here the worker asked Tom to find the softest and the roughest material in a bag, which was filled with materials of many different textures, without looking inside. In putting his hand into the bag, Tom took a risk. He experienced fear, anxiety, tension and possibly a sense of excitement.

These rituals and games eased the way as Tom struggled, bit by bit, with the reality that he could not return to his mother. He began to hope for an adoptive family. In preparing a family, the worker drew on her knowledge of the particular ways that an adult could help Tom feel relaxed and nurtured. Tom also experienced an adult who attended to him, nurtured, cared for and reassured him – in essence, his internal working model of abusive experience and poor sense of self was challenged by the constant repetition of the arousal–relaxation cycle.

Early nurture play

Preparation for permanence can include providing the child with a positive experience of dependence with a nurturing adult. Many children in care have learned to be extremely self-reliant; many are understandably afraid to risk placing their trust in adults when they have been deeply hurt and disappointed. As the number of children who enter the care system as a result of family alcohol and substance misuse increases, they bring particular experiences with them – of being overly self-sufficient, a carer to adults or extremely scared. Children who have fallen back on their own resources to survive find it hard to be nurtured and present a challenge to willing carers eager to care for them. Children who have become carers to their siblings whilst at home may challenge the role of their carers as the child's sense of identity as being competent, grown-up and responsible is threatened. Carers

need help from their supervising social worker or adoption social worker to manage this. Good dialogue between the adult's social worker and the child's social worker is very important in bringing these issues into the open and working towards understanding and planning for them.

Workers and carers can use play to help the child to safely experience vulnerability and dependence and understand that dependence on adults to meet needs is acceptable and safe. Experiencing the acceptance of this in play with an adult creates a safer possibility for risking the building of a relationship outside of the play. The experience of being attended to in play, cared for and cared about can begin to challenge the child's self-concept as unloved and unlovable. Workers can provide re-nurturing experiences in various ways.

Can you care for me? Baby visits the zoo: Lyndsay

Lyndsay was 10 years old when referred for help to establish her relationship with her single kinship carer, Uncle Michael. She had some play sessions with the worker where she had played "house" and had experienced being the director of her own play and acceptance and naming of her feelings. She came to her fourth play session with the worker and asked if Uncle Michael could join in. This was accepted. She had a plan, and sorted out all the wild animals, fences, trees and miniature buckets and brooms from the play box – and added a tiny baby doll. She rummaged through the dressing up box and found a cap, which she gave to Uncle Michael, and a feather boa and a hat, which she put on herself. She told the worker to watch and after putting all the lions, tigers and gorillas in pens, gave Uncle Michael the bucket and broom and some playdough food, telling him he was the zookeeper and had to take care of the fiercest animals and she was visiting the zoo with her baby.

Uncle Michael, in a very attuned and responsive way, set about cleaning up the pen, and talking to and feeding the animals, whilst Lindsay watched from a distance with the baby. Suddenly and without warning, she threw the baby to Uncle Michael, telling him to catch it. Fortunately he did! Uncle Michael quickly realised what

Lyndsay needed and soothed the baby, acknowledging that she was a scared baby and needed to be looked after, and began looking for something to wrap her in and something for her to drink. Lyndsay observed intently for a few minutes and then decided it was time to go home.

The baby basket: Susie

Susie, a 10-year-old girl who suffered severe physical abuse when she was six, was an inquisitive, active child who generally had difficulty focusing on one thing at a time. In the playroom, she would touch every toy and get her hands into everything. On the third visit by a social worker, Susie seemed interested in babies, asking questions about what they ate and played with, so the worker brought a baby basket to the next session. In the basket were a baby blanket, baby powder, lotion, oil, a rattle, a soft duck toy, a baby T-shirt, booties and a bottle. Susie was intrigued by the basket and wanted to know what everything was as she touched things one by one. She and her worker smelled everything and put the oil, lotion and powder on their faces, necks and hands. Susie wanted to explore everything. After a while, she began to talk baby talk. The worker and Susie discussed what babies do, such as babble, wet, cry and drink from a bottle. When Susie saw the bottle, she excitedly said in a loud voice: 'What are we going to do with that?' She soon wanted to suck on the bottle and did.

Susie easily slipped into baby talk and behaviour as a result of the smells and sensations of the baby products. The worker created a nurturing environment which permitted this brief return to infancy. It enabled Susie to experience the dependency of infants and to begin to contrast the needs of babies with the lack of care she herself had received. The early needs that Susie was experiencing were accepted and affirmed, which enabled Susie to explore further and to feel what it may be like to be nurtured by a loving adult. Susie soon gave up the bottle and later turned to her new family for nurturing. The baby basket experience was discussed with her new adoptive family, who recognised Susie's need to be babied and pampered sometimes, even though she seemed too old for this ●

It can be very distressing for carers to see their child regress to very early stages. It is tempting to hurry them out of this phase, or to be concerned that the regression will last or that it is "inappropriate behaviour", or for other siblings to find it embarrassing or funny. It is very important that the carer's support worker contains these feelings for the family and offers supportive reassurance and an explanation of what is going on for the child. As with all play, once needs are met or the child experiences mastery, the play will fall away or move to something else.

Storytelling

Reading a story at bedtime or any other time is an opportunity for closeness and warmth between a child and adult and an activity that both will enjoy and value. For most children this is a routine activity that can continue as a bedtime ritual for many years. However, children in care may need persistence and patience to learn to enjoy this experience. Bedtime may be extremely difficult for such children because it is a reminder of separation and loss. Once reading to the child is established, it can provide a wind-down time during the day or an opportunity to talk or cuddle.

Reading to David

David, an aggressive and overactive 12-year-old, had trouble focusing on any activity for more than a few minutes. His worker discovered that he really relaxed and quietened down when she read stories to him. One of his favourites was a book which seemed more appropriate for a two-year-old than for a 12-year-old. He liked having it read to him over and over again, just as a much younger child would.

Through the reading of baby books, David's worker discovered a technique that an adoptive family could use to help calm David down. She also learned that David was a much better reader than staff believed. His interest in books suggested greater potential in his functioning than was previously thought.

Example of a storyboard

A main character	A task or problem or challenge	Things/people that help the character to cope
This is your hero – your description can be as close to the child as you like – including looks, clothing, hobbies, favourite things	This can be a description of experiences or a metaphor for the experiences, for example, lost toy, scary dragons	This can be strengths, skills or magical objects or people
Things that cause the character difficulty	How the character copes with or tackles the challenges	What happens after the problem is dealt with
Can be places, people or things – best to stay in the metaphor of the child's story than to be explicit	The unique competence, skills or capabilities that the hero has forgotten he had or discovers he has; can include helpers	How it works out in the end for the hero and his helpers

More about story making

Making a story for a child can bring enormous benefits because the writer can appeal to the child in metaphor. The child can become the hero of the story and overcome obstacles, monsters and villains, can problem-solve, feel fear, experience praise and have a happy ending – or mourn a sad one.

Adults may have forgotten or lost sight of their creative side and perhaps think they could never engage in creative writing! Professor Mooli Lahad (1992) suggests a six-part story-making method which enables any adult – or child – to write a story.

Every story should have the following elements:

- a main character
- a task or problem to be coped with
- things that help the character cope
- things that cause the character more difficulty
- how the character copes with the task or problem
- what happens after the problem is dealt with

Try making a storyboard by using the framework in the example storyboard above.

Why is story making so powerful?

All cultures have stories. Story making traditionally carries themes of good and bad, loss and discovery, heroes and villains – in stories, anything can be and anything can happen. In stories, a child can explore a belief system, develop social skills, use their imagination and rational and cognitive skills, and endow themselves with physical power. Story making brings adult and child together in the shared and equal task of containing the child's experience and making meanings and possibilities. The worker who knows the reality of the child's story may make conscious links as the story unfolds. It is helpful if the story can be delivered or received with empathy rather than in a "teaching" or directive style – the child can then experience an affirmation of their experience

Continuity work

Another aspect of babyhood which is disturbed for many children in foster care is the experience of constancy and continuity. When emotional warmth, affection, nurture, good care and enjoyment of the child are available in the child's environment in a constant and predictable way, the feelings associated with the relationship are taken in by the child and become constant and permanent for him. Children who have experienced unpredictability and harm in their early lives cannot hold on to good experiences with others, and therefore trust can become a major issue.

Children who have experienced multiple separations from carers may not believe in the permanence of relationships – a plan for permanence or a "forever family" will be meaningless to them. Furthermore, children in the care system have few concrete reminders of earlier experiences, such as photos, old report cards, souvenirs, baby books and toys; they may also have a fragile sense of the permanence of things in the world. Nor do they have access to a narrative history or bank of family stories or anecdotes about themselves, which can serve to validate and affirm their reality, their sense of self and identity, cultural traditions and sense of belonging to a family or community.

It is necessary to work with the child to enhance their sense of continuity and permanence of possessions, places and people. The **"treasure box"** is used to establish a safe place for things important to the child, and the **"wishing candle"** can be used as a ritual for celebrating special events and dreams for the future.

The treasure box: James

James, an extremely overactive eight-year-old, was living in a children's home. He had previously been hospitalised following a suicide attempt and episodes of confused and extremely challenging behaviour. He had spent his first five years with a drug-addicted mother moving between a variety of temporary accommodations; James was usually very aggressive and had poor impulse control in education and in one-to-one sessions. As a result of his outbursts, his possessions regularly got damaged or destroyed. His worker promised to bring a special box which James could use to keep things which were important to him.

Worker: *Here is the treasure box I promised for things that are important to you. (Gives James a shoe box decorated with tissue paper.)*

James: *(Opens box and looks inside.) There's a leaf inside and a little acorn!*

Worker: *Yes, they can remind us of the work we do together this autumn.*

The worker told James she would hold on to the box until it was time to move or to stop work together and asked him if he had anything from his children's home he would like to keep in it. At first, James had nothing to put in the box.

During each session, the worker would bring out the treasure box and James would look inside. Sometimes, the worker would put an unusual stone or pine cone or a sweet in the box, and James looked forward to the surprise. They kept photos and drawings and small toys in it. In one session, in which James was engaged in work to alert his sense of touch, he grabbed a square of soft red cloth and claimed it for his treasure box.

Worker: *That is important to you, James.*

James: *It's like my...the blanky I had with my mum.*

Worker: *That must have been a special blanket.*

Over time, the treasure box acquired special meaning for James. It was a container for feelings, experiences and memories – both new and old. The box became connected with the nurturing his worker provided him; and it represented the valuable and important aspects of him ●

Children need to experience all parts of themselves – the happy, sad, pleasing, grumpy, irritable, hostile, rejecting, fearful, loving parts. Children, like adults, are multifaceted but those who have experienced harm may more often show their defensive, avoidant or dismissing parts. To have all parts accepted and still be liked and loved challenges the child's perception of adults and of the world. This can lead to emotional healing as all parts of the self are integrated into a core sense of self. When the core self is strengthened, the child's resilience can develop so that, when he is feeling unlovable, he

can know that this is only one part of himself and there are other parts of him too. Even more important is the acceptance and loving of even the unlovable parts of the child in a caring family or an accepting and respectful relationship with a worker. This relationship experience can provide the bridge to a sense of permanence in a family and its influence should not be underestimated. Sadly, a training message often given to carers and workers is that they should not become too attached to a child or facilitate the child's attachment. This stance would seem to affirm the vulnerable child's internal working model rather than challenge it.

PHOTO © HELEN JOUBERT

The wishing candle: Diane

Diane, aged 11, spent her early years with substance-misusing parents and, as a result, was in residential care. She had experienced several placement breakdowns as a result of her aggressive and self-destructive outbursts. She presented as sullen, angry and withdrawn.

As described in Chapter 4, Diane responded well to the sensory experiences of applying scented lotion to her hands, and in later sessions her worker continued to help her to use all her senses to experience the world and to help her build continuity through the treasure box and a ritual called the "wishing candle". The candle was introduced by placing it in the treasure box for her to find during her play session.

Worker: *This candle is your wishing candle. Whenever we celebrate something special together, we're going to light the candle and make a wish. Let's start today because I want to make a wish about the two of us working together. I wish we'll work out where you'll move next and I wish that we will work well together. (Worker blows out the candle and then lights it a second time for Diane to blow out.) Would you like to make a wish now?*

Diane did not make any wishes for several weeks until, at New Year, she said that she wanted to make her first wish. She wished she would find an adoptive family this year. It took Diane several months to verbalise these feelings but, helped by the wishing candle and the predictability and constancy of her relationship with her worker, Diane was able to express some hope for the future. When she eventually met her adoptive family, Diane was open to transferring the trust she had developed with the worker to her new parents ●

In ancient Japanese tradition, wishes were believed to come true if written down and stored in a special wishing pot. Beautifully crafted wishing pots were made from stoneware or porcelain and decorated with lucky symbols. Wishing pots are available on the internet and can be left in the playbox to provoke interest from children, which can then lead to an invitation for the child to try it.

The lost object

Children and young people may make a special connection with a baby toy or other object which seems to symbolise their need for nurturing, caring and constancy. The special object may enable the child to restore symbolically some of the experiences or desires missed in early life. Allowing an older child to play with baby toys also seems to help the independent, guarded child recognise his own needs for the stability and nurture that a permanent family can provide.

The lost object: Jason and Ashley

When he arrived at the family centre, 14-year-old Jason discovered a large stuffed toy dog in the playroom. He stroked it and played with it, just as a younger child would. He could not recall ever having his own stuffed toy, although he had always wanted one. To his delight, his link worker bought him his own on his fifteenth birthday. Jason was very protective of his toy at his group home and cuddled it often.

Ashley, aged eight, chose a soft toy seal for his "lost object". Like Jason, he took great care of his toy and pretended to feed it, comfort it, and put it to bed, demonstrating his own developing capacity for nurture and empathy.

For Jason and Ashley, the lost object perhaps represented their youngest part which craved affection and security. The lost object symbolically replaced some of the nurturing they had missed in their critically formative early years ●

When a child plays consistently with an object, e.g. a piece of fabric which becomes a mask, a blanket, a cleaning cloth or a cover, it is likely that the child has found meaning or has projected meaning onto it, and it should be looked after with care. It is important that the child is not pressured to disclose the meanings; in fact, they may not even be consciously aware of them. However, the worker can name and validate the importance of the object. Objects that have stayed with the child through a number of separations or transitions are very important as they can represent a thread of continuity and predictability in chaotic times.

The lost object: Janie

Janie was reticent about discussing the experiences she had when living with her birth parents. However, when she found a soft toy kitten in the toy box, she remembered a similar toy which was important to her as a small child and this led to a remembering of other things, enabling her to experience and voice her sadness.

Communicating in this way, through the metaphor of a toy or valued object, provides a safe container to talk about powerful feelings, particularly if the adult is very attuned to the child's metaphor. Having found a link to something she had lost, Janie was able to tell the worker about some of her favourite toys as a small child. She talked about a soft toy kitten with a pink nose that she missed very much. The kitten was Janie's lost object. It stood for an object which had accompanied her through her early years, was linked with whatever nurturing her mother had been able to give, and was now a link with the worker who helped her to find another soft toy kitten. Eventually, the kitten accompanied Janie to her adoptive home.

5 Exploring family relationships through play

Older children who have been in the care system for a long time will probably have experienced moves to a number of families, and their understanding of rituals and routines may be very confused. The worker will want to understand the child's perception of what a family is and their hopes for their own future family.

Most children and young people can explore their feelings about families through play and creative activity where they may re-enact some of the parent–child interactions they have experienced in the past. Play functions to explore fantasy and reality and if the worker has developed a good relationship with the child, she can become instrumental in accepting and affirming the exploration of memories of family, and wishes and fears about permanence in a family.

Children who have had intensely impactful experiences can become "stuck" in one type of play as they try to rework or master their trauma. These play activities can provide information which helps workers to assess children's experience, but they need to be helped to resolve their inability to move on, and to be aided in moving to healthy and more spontaneous play.

The worker may suggest alternative activities to move the play forward or to help when it is stuck. Any offer of an alternative or suggestion of a game should be made in a tentative way, leaving the final choice with the child. Remember, it is free play which encourages spontaneity and creativity, which ultimately builds feelings of autonomy, security and self-esteem. Play allows children to feel good about themselves and to learn to engage with others. If the play is consistently repetitive and appears to be distressing to the child, she may be stuck in traumatic play and need help from a play therapist. A worker experiencing this with a child should seek consultation.

Focusing creative play on family and future permanence

One of the simplest forms of creative play is drawing. Many children enjoy drawing pictures of their birth family and/or their imaginative permanent family doing something together. Drawings are a means of communication which can help workers identify whom the children consider to be family, and how they imagine themselves in another family. Workers familiar with using drawings as projective tests can obtain rich diagnostic information from this and other drawing tasks.

The Squiggle game

The Squiggle game was used extensively by Winnicott, who warned against using it as an interpretive tool, but did value the game as an interactional tool in a first meeting with a child. A psychoanalyst *may* use the technique extensively and draw interpretations from the number of squiggles. Workers who are not trained in this work should avoid interpreting the result of the game and instead use it as a means of connecting with and attuning to the child.

The squiggle is casually introduced in the first session as a shared game between child and worker. The worker draws a random squiggle on a piece of paper and the child then makes it into a picture, and then does the same for the worker. Besides drawings, there are other forms of creative play which can be adapted for preparing children for transition.

Building a home: Kasim

Kasim, aged seven, had been in foster care for a year as a result of his parents' separation early in his life and his mother's subsequent mental health issues. Kasim came to his session and asked for a box and extra strong tape and glue from which he fashioned a house.

As he worked, he determined that he would put extra tape on all the walls to make the house strong, but that he would have no windows or doors. As he made his house with the help of the worker, he talked about the furniture needed to make a house comfortable and fashioned a bed, a chair, a lamp, a TV and a pet to take care of and to 'keep him company'. He worked with great urgency to complete the house and was proud and excited to take it home and show his carer. A day later, his social worker phoned the worker to say Kasim was remembering things that had happened with his mother. With support for his carer who played "house" with him, Kasim was able to explore his experiences with his mother and develop a narrative of his life story. The experience was invaluable to his carer who was enabled to empathically understand her foster child's history as he began his long-term placement with her.

This is an example of the child knowing just what he needs to do in order to make sense of his history.

Drawing your adoptive family: Rhys

Rhys was 13 years old at the time of his play therapy. When he was five, he was the youngest of a large group of siblings placed in foster care. Later, he came to a children's home because of explosive and dysregulated behaviour in a series of foster homes. Staff wanted him to move to a permanent family, but knew that Rhys still hoped to return home.

After several meetings in which Rhys expressed a cautious interest in permanence, the worker asked him to draw the family he hoped for. He drew a family of parents and three children with himself in the middle. This appeared to represent the family he knew and was familiar with. The worker noticed that everybody in that family had a smile, much like the smile Rhys himself had. As the worker tracked the progress of the drawing, she expressed her curiosity about the smiling family, thus enabling Rhys to contemplate this too. Knowing Rhys's family history, the worker pondered how difficult it must be to keep smiling when things get very tough and children are angry and upset. As Rhys appeared to be listening, she went on to suggest that perhaps it was really important not to get angry or upset in this family because frightening things would happen. In this activity, the worker hypothesised that Rhys was frightened of angry, negative feelings – his own and those of others – in close family relationships. Rhys had lived in an environment where feelings were subdued by alcohol and children were cared for by older children who hit them if they did not keep quiet. Rhys had a blueprint or fixed idea of what family was, based in harming and trauma. Until this was resolved, he could not think about another family – he was stuck – but this had been mistaken as a wish to return home.

In contrast, when asked to draw "your family" Rhys drew a simple scene of "Rhys and little brother", full of warm, happy feelings. Rhys needed to talk more about his memories of his birth family and begin to work on his life story book, knowing that a permanent family would want to know about his memories. It is important to enquire gently about such pictures and here the worker would learn more about the relationship between Rhys and his brother, providing valuable child-centred information which could help in decision-making about contact plans.

Floor games

Being with children in play does not require a large amount of space or equipment. A worker can create a play space on a mat or blanket which establishes the boundaries of the play world. The worker and the child play together on the floor with toys, including miniature people and animal figures. It is helpful to have a diverse selection of people figures representing ethnicity, gender, age, occupation and disability. Animals should be represented by farm and domestic animals and

PHOTO © ANDREW HAIG ASSOCIATES

fierce jungle or wild animals, including creepy-crawly insects or reptiles. Mythical creatures, for example, dragons or witches, stimulate imagination, and fighting figures and dinosaurs can give outlet to angry and aggressive feelings. In creating a small world on the floor, you will want to have houses, trees and vehicles, including rescue cars and spaceships. Rules should be minimal to help establish a sense of freedom for the play, allowing the child to use his imagination freely.

Floor games: Richie

Richie was a 12-year-old child who lived in a children's home and was about to move to a foster family. The worker initiated a variety of activities in early sessions, including the fantasy holiday trip (see Chapter 3) and simple card games. These activities, along with her regular presence and the way in which she attended to the play, helped the worker and Richie to establish permissiveness in the play.

In the third session, Richie picked up a little girl figure and put it in a casket. He then put a baby in a casket, and tried to put a father figure in a casket but it would not fit. He turned his attention then to two soldiers, a green dinosaur, a primitive bird, a lion and a fox and indicated to

the worker to choose toys too. The worker chose two acorns, a shell, a cat, a tree, a mother figure, a father figure and a magic wand. Richie began the play.

Richie: *(The fox says to the soldier) What are you doing? (The soldier replies) Playing in the woods. (The lion says to the father figure) What are you doing?*

Worker: *(The father says) Playing in the desert.*

Richie: *Now it's your turn.*

The *worker repeated the dialogue of Richie's play with the toys she had chosen.*

(Richie walks his dinosaur to the mother and she acts scared and runs behind the father figure and Richie flies the bird overhead.)

Richie: *(The soldier says) I'm looking for dinosaurs.*

(The dinosaur hides behind the mother and father. The soldier kills the mother and father and dinosaur. The bird kills the soldier and eats him up.)

The game lasted ten minutes and Richie was focused in the play throughout – more focused than the worker had ever seen him before ●

The worker's thoughts:

Starting with placing the family figures in the caskets, Richie's play seemed to reflect the loss he was experiencing through the recent termination of parental rights. Richie's dinosaur sought protection from the mother and father figures, but all of them were killed in the end.

In the metaphor of the play, Richie began to express some of his feelings of loss and violation. In subsequent sessions, the worker was able to reflect and name the feelings in the play, thereby giving Richie the words to express his emotional distress, and at the same time giving him an experience of the power of empathy. She did not direct the play or evaluate it, nor did she terminate it or show disapproval of the aggression. The permissiveness helped Richie to explore his angry and distressed feelings further without any sense of rejection from the worker.

Sessions such as this show that the child will face issues that they can manage. Richie was not yet ready to discuss moving to another family – he still had work to undertake on his grief, and he used future play sessions to continue to work out these feelings. Although the worker tried other activities, Richie was most drawn to floor games and spontaneously asked to play again and again as he explored his experiences and integrated and resolved his feelings about them. This play ultimately led to life story work (see Chapter 6).

Despite the restricted nature of the play, it was an opportunity for Richie to become more open as his confusion was resolved. During this time, the worker saw other sides of Richie, who was generally overactive, aggressive and difficult to manage. She could then help staff and an adoptive family better empathise with his worries and later help him to express them more directly.

The little war game: Sean

Sean, aged nine, displayed extremely distressed and challenging behaviour. There was great anxiety about him because of his self-harming behaviour and his aggression towards others. He was regarded as hyperactive and difficult to contain. Sean was at risk of placement breakdown and it became imperative to help him. In floor play, he selected fences, stones, trees, houses, horses, jeeps and helicopters, and created aggressive weapons from materials in the playroom. Sean's challenging behaviour meant that it was important to negotiate ground rules,

particularly about setting limits. The worker told Sean at the beginning of each session that he could do *almost anything*, but if there was something he wasn't allowed to do, she would tell him. Being used to tight rules, Sean was surprised by this, and he responded by adding his own rules.

- Only move one figure for each turn.

- When a soldier falls on his back, he's dead and goes to the graveyard, and when he falls on his face, he's wounded and goes to the hospital.

- The person who has the most soldiers standing by the end of the time is the winner.

Sean set up the figures and added some protective barriers, such as stones and walls.

Sean: *I'll go first. This knight is a scout, and he sneaks up behind the rock to see what your army is doing. He has a walkie-talkie and can tell the captain over here what's going on. Now it's your turn.*

The worker chose the knights and placed them as Sean had done around the walls.

Sean: *This man gets on the horse and rides behind your army. He sees this soldier standing alone and knocks him out. (Soldier falls on face.)*

Sean wanted to play the "little war game" during every session. Judging that Sean was needing structure and predictability, the worker established a routine of play for 15 minutes – a sufficient length, because the play was arousing for Sean as he fought battles and vanquished foes. After this, they would change to an activity which was more relaxing, such as sharing a snack or story, followed by another activity enabling Sean to play, explore or continue to relax. In this the worker was gently establishing the arousal, soothe and explore cycle that Sean needed to differentiate between heightened and relaxed feelings, and gradually enabled him, through more sustained play, to experience all parts of himself as a happy, sad, excited, fearful, brave victim and hero.

At a cognitive level, this experience of floor play encouraged Sean to follow rules and plan ahead. It was fun for him and helped build his self-confidence, while teaching him a positive way to channel his aggressive energies. The relationship with his worker felt safe because it was permissive and accepting, but with a rule he could remember – he could do almost anything and if there was something he could not do she would tell him. This helped him to move to an emotionally safer and more trusting position, in which he could engage in creative activities where he played out the understanding of how relationships worked – learned in his family and quite possibly in his residential establishment.

Playing in the sand and the world in miniature

Sand play is a psychotherapeutic technique initiated by the Freudian psychiatrist Margaret Lowenfeld and adapted using Jungian symbology by Dora Kalff.

The Lowenfeld technique (see http://therapist4me.com/sandtray%20therapy.htm) requires two wooden trays (size 18" x 27" x 2") with waterproof liners filled with sand – one is used for dry sand, the other for wet sand. Small objects which represent real and imagined people and things are arranged on narrow book shelves behind the trays. Children are free to play with the objects and sand.

Spaulding workers adapted this technique for adoption preparation and assessment purposes. Sometimes children made a picture or a scene using figures of their choice; sometimes they played with objects in the sand; and sometimes workers gave children specific figures to play with. When it was impossible to bring children to the playroom where the sand trays were located, workers encouraged children to play with the miniature objects on a small blanket on the floor.

In the early phases of play, staff found that children frequently act out war scenes or fights and that this can be thought of as the testing for protection stage of the play – when the child is beginning to explore her relationship with the worker and perhaps testing if the worker can tolerate what for the child are overwhelming and frightening feelings. After this stage, when feelings have been accepted, children may then begin playing out family relationships, transitions, hopes and fears, and also expressing thoughts, dreams and feelings.

Play in the world in miniature or the sand tray can lead the child to ask questions about their life history, which should be recorded in their life story book. Therapeutic play and life story work can support each other in this way.

As with other play techniques, minimal interpretation of children's play is recommended. Workers may reflect the theme of the play story back to the child and will often reflect the feelings that are being expressed in the play. "Why" questions need rarely, if ever, be asked, since this puts children in the position of having to change into cognitive thought from imaginative thought, and formulating an answer can interrupt the flow of the experience. Be mindful too that the questions are often more for the benefit of the worker than the child! Workers can express an interest in the child's activity by naming, feeling or tracking the process of the play and show that they are attending to the child. The child may spontaneously talk about the pictures they have made or describe what the characters are doing, and this is easier for the child if she is not questioned about them.

Sand tray work: Janie

Janie, aged 10, was separated from parents who misused alcohol to the point that it affected their parenting capacity, and Janie was taken into care. Her social worker believed that she was uncertain about being adopted and was silently mourning her parents. The goals of work with Janie were to help her discuss her feelings of loss and sadness about her past. Janie was friendly and mildly accepting of the idea of another family, but she seemed low in energy and in spontaneity, probably grieving for her parents, but not willing to talk about this. The worker offered her a variety of miniature figures to use to tell a story. Janie accepted eagerly, playing on the floor with the worker nearby.

Janie created an orderly world of a village, with a house nestled under some trees, babies in their cribs, etc. She then drove a car through the village wildly, destroying everything. She said she would put things 'in their right places' next time. She did just that in the next session, magically restoring the village to its original state. As the worker named the confusion and muddle that was present in the play, commenting that Janie had made a village where everything was in order and then it got spoiled, Janie began to talk a little about what she missed in her old family life, and it was at this point that she talked about missing her little soft toy kitten with the pink nose. The kitten proved to be a significant lost object for Janie (see Chapter 4), perhaps representing all the other losses she had experienced in her life. In grieving for her kitten, she experienced some of the feelings of loss and these were named by the worker, which gave Janie the language to help her express her other losses too. As she became less stuck in her overwhelming feelings, she was free to progress her play and process her experiences.

In later sessions, Janie used the sand tray to construct a scene in which a "quiet village" gets buried; she tried to dig it out, but could not. Afterwards, she asked why she could not go back to her parents. In the next session, Janie created a desert scene in the sand, which turned into a landscape of hills and lakes, and then was flooded and destroyed. Janie tried to save a little figure, but it got buried in the sand. In the following sessions, Janie did not want to return to the sand tray, but became interested in the baby dolls. Janie talked about some happy times from her childhood, which perhaps served to strengthen her for the more painful memories she explored later. Freed from feeling lost and overwhelmed, she was able to reconstruct some of her more difficult family history through play.

When the worker offered Janie a chance to write "The story of Janie" for her life story book, Janie went back to the miniature figures to tell some of the story. She acted out with toy figures a scene in which her parents were drunk and she was on her own. Janie used a policeman puppet to beat up the "parent" dolls. In this way, she was able to express her anger with her parents, without the subsequent guilt which may have followed if she had spoken directly about this.

In these ways, Janie was helped to move gradually through despair and to talk about her hopes to return to her parents. The worker was then able to talk to her about why this was not possible.

Eventually, Janie was ready to look forward to an adoptive family. She showed through play what she needed from an adoptive family – a family who could meet her "baby" needs. Creating a scene with the miniature figures, she had the "Janie" figure jump into the crib and displace the baby of the hypothetical adoptive family. This was a clear message, which the worker made sure to pass along to the family which eventually adopted Janie.

The world in miniature: Jamal

Jamal, a ten-year-old boy with learning difficulties and an expressive language delay, lived in a residential home for children with developmental disabilities. He was withdrawn and uncommunicative with all but one or two staff members. He had been physically abused by his birth family and had lived in the home since he was removed from his family at an early age. Residential staff believed that Jamal had no memories of his family life and his early experiences were not discussed with him because workers thought he would not understand or remember them.

Jamal generally seemed preoccupied. He made little eye contact with his adoption worker and made minimal responses to verbal communication from her, but he did like to play with miniature figures. In the first play session, Jamal played with people figures, developing a story of a baby who was getting beaten up by the mother and was then rescued by a superhero figure. In the second play session, Jamal continued with the play people and became engrossed in his play with them. He was able to engage with his worker, making brief requests of the worker to help him make the objects he needed, such as a house, a car, etc. Jamal played out conventional family activities, showing a good deal of knowledge of what it is like to live in a family, although the worker noticed there was very little engagement with the mother figure. What was interesting for the worker and assisted her understanding of Jamal's experience was her observation that, in the play, the mother was never closely involved with the son, but there were a few moments when the father took the son's hand and they went off together.

Upon arriving for the next session, Jamal, unusually, looked directly at the worker and asked for the toys. From this point, the worker encouraged him to look at her when he talked. Jamal was able to make better eye contact and spontaneously added "please" to his requests.

In the following session, the worker attempted to start "The story of Jamal" as a preliminary to life story work. Jamal was fascinated with pasting his picture on the cover of the life story book and writing his name under it. However, when the worker spoke of Jamal as a baby, and wanted to put a drawing of "Baby Jamal" in the book, he protested 'No! no! no!' vigorously. Later that day, Jamal went to his key worker and asked to see pictures of himself as a baby.

The worker's new attempts to involve Jamal in looking at early photos and discussing his pre-institutional days were not productive. Jamal preferred to play intensely with baby figures and nursery furniture. He always added a mummy and a daddy who were sometimes kind and caring with the babies, but soon went off dancing, came back and scolded the babies harshly, spanked them and argued over who should look after them. Jamal repeated this play a number of times and the worker tracked the play and finally spoke about how hard it must be for the babies to feel that no one wanted them. After this session, Jamal again asked his carer what he was like as a baby. Could he be working out if he was loveable?

This process of play in the world in miniature enabled Jamal to explore his dreams, nightmares and fantasies in the supportive, non-invasive presence of the worker. It provided the worker with information about his perceptions of the world and his place in it. It helped the worker learn the gaps in Jamal's knowledge of his past and assess his beliefs about himself and what mums and dads did for you, and how this might affect his ability to fit into a family.

Play activities with Jamal showed, among other things, his internal working model of a parenting figure. Such richness of information and understanding would have been lost if the worker had persisted in showing photos and talking about them. Jamal's play had helped the worker understand that the task for Jamal's carers was re-parenting to lay down a healthier internal working model of being given and receiving good care.

Jamal's relationship with his worker was equally important in modelling a playful, accepting, curious and empathic presence in his life. He began to respond more to the worker as she reached out warmly and continuously to him. He finally left the projective play with figures and moved to exploratory and active movement in the park and playground and, using his worker as a secure base, he climbed trees, collected leaves and insects and played ball. He began to stay close to her, and talk for increasing lengths of time about his discoveries as if taking pleasure in communicating by words.

Future work to expand Jamal's potential for attaching to an adoptive parent included re-nurturing activities such as the baby basket (see Chapter 4), as well as an attempt to help residential care staff tell Jamal simply about his mother and her problems with parenting him – something he was clearly asking about through his repeated "family" play.

Sand tray work: Sean

Sean, aged nine, began playing in the sand from the start of the preparation process and continued throughout the period of visiting with his new family and moving in. In the beginning, his stories in the sand were aggressive and involved pushing sand around, piling it up, and burying objects and people. In one session, he buried babies in a playpen. He later put babies in an egg, buried them, and said: 'Babies always want to get dirty. I'll make a big pile.' He threw all the babies and mothers and fathers in the sand.

In the same session, Sean played with a dragon, stuffing sand in his mouth and saying: 'He's throwing up, he ate too much.' The dragon vomited on the father, then hit him. Next Sean took the father, dragon, soldiers, cowboys and animals, and covered them all with sand. He continued to play, lining up all the fierce animals and the monsters and having them fight it out. In this session, Sean's play was extremely chaotic and the final "pictures" in the sand were disorganised and messy looking.

As Sean came closer to moving in with his adoptive family, his play became less aggressive and chaotic, and his stories were more integrated. Now his pictures reflected a preoccupation with orderly feeding and being fed. He began to set up farm scenes in which he was continually feeding babies, animals or himself.

Sean's new focus on nurturing in play was described to the adoptive parents. They began to understand that Sean was asking for some real babying in addition to the regular parenting a nine-year-old requires. With help and support, parents can offer the opportunities in day-to-day care and in special play.

6 Life story work

In recent years, children's rights, underpinned by the United Nations Convention of the Rights of the Child (UNCRC) (ratified 20 November 1989) have been increasingly promoted. Though not yet legally binding in the UK, these rights do create a set of recognised standards that are often referred to by national and international courts and bodies.

Article 7 determines that children have the right to a legally registered name and nationality and the right to know and, as far as possible, to be cared for by their parents. Article 7 states Parties undertake to respect the right of the child to preserve his or her identity, including nationality, name and family relations as recognised by law without unlawful interference.

Article 12 asserts the importance of participation, ensuring that children and young people have the *right* to say what they think should happen to them in any decision-making process and to have their decisions taken into account in accordance with their age and maturity.

Article 8 promotes respect for the right of the child to *preserve his or her identity,* including nationality, name and family relations as recognised by law.

The life story process is part of the exercise of rights upheld by the UNCRC and thus is a priority activity if children are to be treated equally and protected from harm.

The life story work process serves two main purposes. The first is to assist the child in integrating their past, present and future. Some of the techniques described in previous chapters help the child to communicate about the past, construct a more positive self-image, and begin to aspire to a more fulfilling future, and this could also be said of life story work. However, the second purpose of life story work is to gather photographs, mementoes and important objects, and to document the work completed by the child and worker during the assessment, planning and preparation process, and to write the story so that it can be communicated to the child in a meaningful way. The life story process can be viewed as both a "product" and a "process". (Ryan and Walker (2007) present a rich and creative assortment of useful techniques and exercises for adults doing life story work with children in different settings. They also examine and discuss the use of various new interactive media in life story work.) Life story work is a process which integrates the child's past with their present to make sense of where the child is. However, it is also about future aspirations and hopes. It should be an integral part of the planning and preparation process, but is too often sidelined or left waiting. Edith Nicholls (2005) offers helpful resources on completing life story work in a thorough, systematic and helpful way, with follow-up resources in the form of memory books for different ages of children.

Children have powerful ties to their birth parents, regardless of their experiences of parents who abuse or neglect them but, as we have witnessed, the child's internal world (thoughts, wishes, beliefs) will affect his capacity to make sense of his experience. The process of life story work focuses on the child's understanding of the past and present, which pays attention to the child's perceptions, allows for ambiguity and contradictions, and enables exploration of the child's story as an ongoing process.

The life story process can help because it looks at the people in the child's life, what happened to the child and the reasons why those things happened. The narratives of our looked after children are increasingly complex and their life story cannot simply be a book with basic narrative or description. Life story work can be a therapeutic tool and an opportunity to help the child connect their inner and outer experiences. It can facilitate an experience of attachment with a worker and increase trust for an adult who works with and validates the child's experiences and who helps the child recognise and resolve strong emotions related to past life events.

All children need a chronology of their life which can help them to share their history with others. It is usually parents who hold such a chronology but for children separated from their birth parents and who have had a number of carers, it becomes imperative to record the facts. If a child is very young or emotionally or psychologically not able to manage the life story work process, it is still important to bring together the facts of his history and to give an accurate account that "makes sense". One has to be wary in trying to make sense in the life story book of sanitising the facts and implicitly suggesting the possibility of reparation and resolution. The life story "book" should identify positives, as well as negatives, about the birth family, in language that is honest and avoids sanitising but which is balanced; the production of a life story book is not an end in itself.

Central to the life story process and book is a sense of who this child is. Knowledge of identity, culture and sense of belonging to a community happens when one is part of a family and a community but for children in transition, their sense of identity can become disjointed and a sense of belonging is never established for them. An awareness of one's ethnic identity and heritage provides a sense of belonging and historical continuity, and denial or neglecting the promotion of this can affect a child's mental health and emotional well-being, deplete their resilience and capacity to cope with racism and cause painful confusion or a sense of isolation.

Children should have the benefit of adults around them who reflect and have an understanding of their culture and language. The involvement of workers who can help with identity and issues of racism and internalised oppression will strengthen the child and promote and preserve their pride and self-esteem, and deal with distancing from their own culture as a result of harm (see Barn (ed), 1999).

Donley's (1987) guidelines outlining major considerations in undertaking life story book work could be useful to readers, and there is much additional literature available describing the use of life story books; some of these are listed in the bibliography.

This chapter provides examples of the major components of life story work and of what

Spaulding termed "disengagement work" and which would now be termed "grief work", or letting go, or being part of the life story work process. This process would include:

- exercises about the past: clarifying and remembering early childhood and developing a written record;

- exercises about the present: reconstructing the child's self-image, identifying loving and giving, and grieving for losses;

- exercises about adoption: education about adoption;

- disengagement work: getting permission to move on.

Exploring the child's past

As a means of opening the child to exercises about the past, *The Suitcase Story*, by Carmela Wenger (1982), is a helpful analogy of the transient lifestyle of foster children and the anger, sadness and frustration which multiple moves can produce. To clarify the child's story for themselves, workers frequently use the life journey chart, a flow chart of all the places a child has lived in and the people who have come into and left their lives. Another technique is to ask children to draw the floor plans of previous homes. Workers may also take the child to neighbourhoods in which the child has previously lived and take photographs of important sites for the life story book whenever possible.

Moving calendar: Matthew

Matthew was 13 when referred to the specialist CAMHS because his behaviour was challenging – he was lying, stealing and running away. His eighth foster placement was in jeopardy. During the first meeting, it was apparent that Matthew would not engage in dialogue but he would draw. In subsequent sessions the worker made sure that a variety of collage materials were available to him. It wasn't long before Matthew

Friday 22nd September		
Friday 29th September		
Friday 6th October		
Tuesday 10th October		Visit to my new School at 10.30 am. Anne and Jane Will take me.
Saturday 14th October		

after much thought drew a shirt hanging on a coat hanger at the bottom of some stairs. He explained – his carer ironed a clean school shirt for him every day. This led to a discussion about what adults can do for children. Matthew began to understand some of his life history and the concept of good care ●

In these exercises about the past, workers try to help children remember both the positive and negative details of their lives and accept these as a part of themselves. Remembering the painful past is difficult, but children do not have to be alone in this as they may have been before. Workers let children explore their memories at their own pace. If a child says 'I don't know' to most questions, a worker may say:

Worker: *That's OK if you don't want to tell me. I need to know if you just don't know, or you just don't want to talk about it right now.*

Child: *I don't want to talk about it.*

Worker: *It's difficult just now. (Child nods.) OK, when you do want to talk about it, you let me know.*

There may be points beyond which the child cannot go and this should be respected. Life story work is important but cannot be "done" to a timescale, and therefore carers and other workers should always be aware of what has been achieved so far.

began to draw family members and talk about them. It was important to Matthew that the worker did not scrutinise him but worked alongside him in his drawing and sticking.

As the holiday season approached, after about seven sessions, the worker made a "moving calendar", with each "door" representing a placement. When Matthew asked what the worker was doing, she told him what it was and that she was making this for him and invited him to colour in the front doors. This led to a discussion about what might be behind each door. For one door, Matthew remembered sitting alone in his bedroom at meal times – as a foster child he was not allowed a pudding. When the worker affirmed his anger about this and acknowledged this should not have happened, Matthew was able to talk about why he ran away from his placement. Finally, he coloured and opened the door to his present placement and

Life journey chart: Marc

Marc, aged nine, was living in a children's home. The staff said that he rarely referred to past families, though he occasionally mentioned "Mummy". The worker began the life journey chart in an early session. She hoped to discover what Marc knew about his early life, and whether he was ready to talk about some of his past relationships. The discussions which follow occurred during several sessions.

The worker suggested they make a drawing of the places Marc had lived. She sketched a hospital and a baby. Marc was interested for a short time but changed the subject. The worker offered some play, and he relaxed. A couple of sessions later, the worker returned to the subject:

Worker: *Let's work some more on the life journey chart. (Draws a series of houses, and points to the last one.) Here's the Brown family, Marc, where you used to live. Who lived in this house?*

Marc: *Mummy…and my father.*

Worker: *Yes, your foster mum and dad. And where did you live before you came to their house?*

Marc: *Nowhere else!*

Worker: *Did you know that you had another mum?*

Marc: *(Shakes his head.) No, I didn't.*

Worker: *You were born to another mum, and both of you started out together in the hospital where you were born. (Writes "hospital" on the first building on the chart.) Her name was Susan.*

Marc: *She was pretty! I remember!*

Worker: *And she tried to take care of you when you were a baby. You went home from the hospital with her, and you lived here for a while. (Drawing the house, and inviting Marc to draw a path from the hospital to the house.)*

Marc: *But she used to drink a lot, and fight with my dad.*

Worker: *So she couldn't take care of you the way a baby needs, even though she tried. And you went to live with your foster mum and dad. (Marc draws path to their house.) Do you want to draw yourself when you were a baby way back here? (Points to the beginning of the chart.)*

(Marc draws a mother holding a baby in a protecting way.)

Worker: *That must be you and your birth mum. You hope that your mum tried to look after you.*

The life journey chart was the basis for some further discussions of Marc's moves. The technique helped Marc open up about the foster family that eventually rejected him, and the adoptive family of his future.

Drawing floor plans: Joe

Joe, aged 11, had been adopted from age five until age ten, when his adoptive placement disrupted. Joe did not like to speak about his family, though he actively participated in non-verbal play related to families. When the time came for clarifying his life story and recalling his experiences with his family, the worker asked Joe to draw the layout of the house where he had lived. Joe drew the floor plans and described the kinds of activities which took place in each room. He was able to express how many good times the family had had together and also how sad he was about the disruption.

The mapping exercise provided an outlet for Joe to express some of the grief he felt at his terrible loss, perhaps even resonant of his first separations. The drawings and the descriptions of Joe's memories were included in his life story book. This is an example of the product of the life story book and the process of life story work coming together in a powerful experience for the child.

Dealing with feelings

The creation of the life story book (or box or CD) is a process which helps the child explore his changing identity and developing self-image and the work will also explore present behaviour. There are many good exercises on identity awareness, self-esteem building and thinking about loving and giving; below are some examples of feelings pictures, feelings faces, the "bottle of loving and giving" activity and the "coat of arms".

Feelings pictures

Worker: *Can you describe what it feels like to be angry?*

Child: *You know, mad.*

Worker: *Yes, but there are different kinds of angry feelings. Let's make a picture of feeling angry (with crayons or in clay). The first one will be when you're so mad you could just burst. The* *second one will be when you're angry at some small thing, maybe you had a little fight with your friend or something, and the anger goes away quickly.*

This exercise can be used to explore other feelings such as sadness or disappointment, anger or guilt. Using feelings faces can be a way of connecting with emotions that a child cannot put into words. The worker draws a circle to represent a face, and asks the child to show what he or she looks like when angry, sad, lonely, happy, etc. Children will readily draw a down-turned mouth or tears on the face, and then can often talk about how they have been feeling or what they got sad or worried about in the past. A pile of paper plates is helpful for drawing and sticking on during this work.

Feelings faces: Ben

This technique was helpful to Ben and his long-term foster carer, who was preparing for his move to an adoptive family. Ben had been angry and provoking with the foster carer since she decided that she would not adopt him herself. Things had become so difficult that the foster carer was asking for his removal.

The worker talked with Ben and his carer about the many different feelings children have about leaving a family. Ben used feelings faces to draw the way he looked in different moods, and what

caused him to feel like this. When they came to "sad", Ben talked tearfully about the many things he had shared with the foster family – the trips, the special meals, etc. The sadness underlying Ben's anger was now clear to the carer. She and Ben had joined in anger, displacing their distress about each other onto the worker and the agency. This did not feel congruent for Ben, who was upset at his carer. Once this was identified and understood by Ben and his carer, they were able to resolve it and end the placement in a meaningful and containing way, as Ben was helped to understand the reasons why he could not remain there. Surviving a planned leaving, in which loss is experienced and empathically contained, develops resilience and is preferable to a child leaving a foster family prematurely because of "bad" behaviour which instils shame and guilt.

Engaging in these two activities before the "bottle of loving and giving" exercise helps to ensure that the child can attach appropriate language to feelings. It is important that the child and worker mean the same or similar things when the language of emotion is used.

The bottle of loving and giving

This exercise can be used with any child to begin work about loving and giving and emotional muddles and the value of expressing emotions. The worker first brings out a small bottle filled with a fizzy drink and a cup.

Worker: *I brought a special bottle today. It's called the bottle of loving and giving. Let's pretend this fizzy drink is loving and giving.*

Other people have loving and giving too…and sometimes yours and their loving and giving can get mixed up. (Pours more drink into cup.) Like when you moved to the Smith family. Mr and Mrs Smith gave you some of their loving and giving (adds drink from the bottle) and you gave them some of yours.

Then, something happened that hurt you very much and your loving and giving got mixed up with sad and angry which sometimes you kept in and sometimes they spilled over like this (shaking the bottle). But that made it even harder so you decided to mostly keep your loving and giving in. (Covers cup with plastic wrap.) Now, nothing can get out of your cup. But perhaps nothing can get in either…

But when somebody wants to give you some of their loving and giving – perhaps that they like you and want to be with you – what happens? (Tries to pour drink from bottle into cup.) See what a mess it makes because it can't get in!

And…if you decide you want to give a little of yours to somebody else (pours from first cup into bottle) it gets hard to let them out…so it feels like nobody understands how things are for you…and the longer it stays like this the harder it gets…like there is more plastic wrap on.

(Worker puts another layer on top of the cup.) Nothing can come in and nothing can go out. (Worker shakes cup and, because the drink is carbonated, it fizzles.) Oops! What happens when you shake this up too much?

Child: *I don't know.*

Worker: *Have you ever opened a fizzy drink when it's been shaken up?*

Child: *Yes! It spurts out all over the place.*

Worker: *Yes, that's like loving and giving and sad and angry too. If they're held inside too long, they get all tossed around and mixed up until they burst out like a fizzy drink does. Even though you think you're holding them in, like with plastic wrap, they're very powerful and escape anyway. We'll take one layer off and see if that makes a difference. Do you think it will?*

Child: *No, you have to take both layers off.*

Worker: *Yes, otherwise you still can't give or get any loving and giving…or let out sad and angry either…so how can anyone know what you feel?*

After this exercise, the worker and child clean up the mess. Later, they work on the life story book and talk about the people who have been loving and giving with the child and who have been angry or frightening too and how this can "go in". Children who have been significantly harmed may have difficulty with the concept of "loving and giving". The worker must be aware that *encouraging* the child to think in this way may feel incongruent and painful to them and lead to self-blame. It could also encourage a sanitised version of the real experience. Feelings are often very muddled for children, who cannot always name them in themselves and therefore find it difficult to receive other people's feelings which can then be perceived as a lack of empathy on the part of the child.

The coat of arms: Tom

Worker: *Do you know what a coat of arms is?*

Tom: *A what?*

Worker: *A coat of arms is a sign which represents important things about you or your family. We're going to make Tom's coat of arms, like this. Let's cut one out of cardboard. You choose the colour…Every person has some things they like and some they don't like. So, on one side we'll put the best things, and on the other side we'll put the others. First, let's write 'The best thing that ever happened' on this side and 'The worst thing that ever happened' on the other side. OK, what's the best thing that ever happened to you?*

Tom: *I don't know.*

Worker: *Has someone been nice to you? Have you done something you've been proud of at school? Have you ever gone to a really wonderful place?*

Tom: *My grandfather bought me a fire engine for my birthday once.*

Tom and his worker completed the coat of arms together. Tom glued it into his life story book and decorated the page using crayons. The exercise helped Tom develop a sense of his own value and importance. It also opened up his feelings about special people in his life.

Additional exercises recommended are a self-collage, which includes images (from magazines) of what a child wants to do for himself, and the "phrase booklet" which lists words and phrases a child uses to help get along with other people.

Inside-outside boxes

This is a powerful exercise for adults and children and is best undertaken when you know the child well. It is beneficial to experience this exercise yourself before offering it to a child.

Requirements: pile of comics, magazines, glitter, coloured paper, collage materials, feathers, etc. A shoe box or large envelope.

Using pictures from the magazines or the material provided, cut out anything that represents what people see on the outside and that you are happy for people to know about you.

Then do the same for the inside box, this time representing private parts of you that only you know about. In here, you might put plans, hopes and dreams – what you like about yourself or what you hate about yourself.

The child does not have to reveal the inner box but this experience may help to bring the unconscious or unspoken into the fore for the child, who may well talk or play out in other sessions.

Thinking about adoption

In their study of children's understanding of adoption, Brodzinsky et al (1984) found that, before the ages of 12 to 14, children do not usually recognise the full legal ramifications of adoption – that adoption involves the legal transfer of rights and responsibilities to adoptive parents.

The authors argue that knowledge of adoption derives from a 'general process of construction and not simply from a gradual accumulation of facts or bits of information presented by parents

and significant others'. They suggest that parents and adults, in spite of attempts to teach this, should not expect a child to understand adoption as a permanent, legal relationship until the child is cognitively mature enough to process this information fully. However, they also suggest that, from the ages of about six to eight, children can begin to differentiate between birth and adoption as alternative ways of entering a family, and that the complexities of their situation begin to emerge for children from about the age of eight.

Especially with older children, it is useful for workers to explain the different kinds of birth, foster and adoptive family relationships, as a means of laying the foundation for a more complete understanding of adoption as the child matures. Workers can build a simple list with the child of the attributes of each type of family and place it in the life story book. Fahlberg (1994, p.149) developed a list of parental roles which has been adapted below.

The genetic inheritance – birth parents

- The gift of life
- Sex determination
- Intellectual potential
- Heritage and cultural identity
- Predisposition for certain diseases
- Personality traits (i.e. shy, stubborn, active)
- Talents

Being protected – legal parents

- Make major decisions (where you live, where you go to school)
- Financial responsibility
- Legally responsible for safety and security
- Give consent for minors (medical consent, marriage consent, driver's license)

Family experience – parenting parents

- Love
- Discipline
- Provide for daily needs (food, clothes, toys)
- Provide for your emotional well-being, sense of self-identity and self-esteem
- Take care of you when you're sick or hurt

- Teach values

- Religious training

- Provide life skills training (how to cook, drive, budget, and care for yourself)

Workers also distinguish between adoptive and foster families by using concrete examples and age-appropriate language, and the following example illustrates this.

Worker: *An adoptive family is a family who want you to be their daughter (or son).*

When you grow up and have your own home, your adoptive family will still be your family. You'll still come to see them, and you'll help each other.

If you have children some day, your adoptive parents will be Grandma and Grandpa to your kids.

After you're adopted, you'll take the same last name as your new family.

When you're adopted, you won't need a social worker anymore. You and your parents can call us only when you want to or need to.

Child: *I was adopted before (referring to a foster family).*

Worker: *That family was a foster family. That's a family you stay with until your social worker can decide on the best plan (family) for you.*

Disengagement work

Many children carry active hopes and sometimes fears of returning to birth family members which, in effect, impede resolution of powerful feelings of anger, sadness and loss. Some children have been told by a parent specifically that they should never be adopted, that they must never change their last name, and that one day their parent will find them and bring them home. Children who maintain unrealisable fantasies of reunions with birth families can often benefit from a "blessing" or confirmation of approval to help them disengage and give the child permission to be adopted. Donley (1987) identifies five steps in this work:

- accurate reconstruction of the child's placement history;

- identification of the various attachment figures in the child's life;

- decisions about the most powerful of the attachment figures or the surrogates;

- gaining the co-operation of the most significant attachment figure available;

- communication of the permission signal to the child.

An aunt, uncle, grandparent, residential social worker or former foster carer – someone whom the child trusts – can empathise with the child's pain and longing, while sending wishes that the child will join a new family.

Help from a foster carer: Rhys

Foster carers are often significant figures in children's lives, offering an experience of being cared for and cared about.

Rhys, a nine-year-old whose family drawings are discussed in Chapter 5, talked about his birth family with longing. In working on his life story book, he also began to refer to his last foster mother, Mrs Watson, and the warmth and caring in her home. In fact, he revealed that he still called her now and again, but had not told her he was thinking about adoption. Rhys still seemed "stuck" in the past, and the worker knew of nobody from his birth family who could give him permission to move on. The worker then turned to Mrs Watson, visited her, and asked for her help.

Rhys and the worker spent an afternoon in Mrs Watson's home. Rhys approached the house with excitement, pleased to show the worker his old neighbourhood. He remembered a short-cut to the house, and then other memories welled up once he and Mrs Watson were together. They talked about the old days and Rhys caught up on news about people he had known. They talked about good times and also about some of Rhys's hard times there. Mrs Watson recalled his regular meetings with his mother, and commented on how sad and upset he always was on coming back from a visit. Mrs Watson let Rhys know she was proud of him and how grown-up she thought he had become. She expressed very clearly that she cared about him and his future, and hoped that he would find adoptive parents.

Rhys got much satisfaction from this contact. After hoping briefly that he could return to Mrs Watson's home, he did in fact open himself to adoption.

Help from a grandmother: Peter

Peter, 13, had lived with a grandmother until he came into foster care at the age of six. Starting permanence preparation work with him, his worker found that he refused to talk about his experiences in his grandmother's home, except to indicate that he was too "bad" to stay with his grandmother. Peter saw the grandmother sporadically, when he pressed for a visit with her. The visits were always upsetting for everyone.

The worker met with the grandmother, who wanted to be helpful to Peter, but didn't want to be responsible for him again. She provided stories of his early days, and early snapshots of Peter and his birth family, which added to his knowledge of them and his sense of identity. However, Peter at first resisted looking at these with the worker. Then, seeing a picture of himself as a toddler, he exclaimed: 'I was really cute!' He studied the photos and began to recall some of the details of living with the grandmother, such as his favourite chair and the games he used to play with his

uncle. In the agency playroom, Peter went on to pick out some soft toy animals and have them represent himself, his grandmother, an uncle, and the connections among them.

In following sessions, Peter at times delighted in the soft toy animals as a much younger child would. He and the worker put the treasured snapshots in an album. He connected more closely to the worker in sharing these experiences. Though still reserved, he would talk in fragments about the past. He began to tell about some of his "bad boy" escapades as a five- and six-year-old. Although he was sensitive to any clarification that sounded like a criticism of his grandmother, he accepted the idea that he had not had a chance to learn how to behave in those days.

The worker met several times with Peter's grandmother during the course of this work. Her care and concern for Peter was genuine. Involving her as a helpful ally resolved her guilt at not being able to care for Peter, and she invited him for some visits, let him know she cared about him, and encouraged him to consider adoption. Peter did begin to imagine an adoptive family for himself. Composing a description for interested families, he referred to himself as a "good boy" who sometimes did bad things – and who needed parents to guide him.

7 Filial therapy: how it can help

Play therapy is an established intervention to support children, and is increasingly used for children in foster care or who are adopted. Many children, especially those who have come into the care system because of experiences suffered in the birth family home, have emotional, behavioural and/or mental health problems. These can prevent them from reaching their full potential, but many children can be helped through play therapy and the creative arts. Modern play therapy is based upon principles developed by Virginia Axline (1947) and has been based on a person-centred approach to therapy with adults. Play therapy is carried out by specially trained professional therapists.

About filial therapy

Communicating with children in essential to the process of planning for them. In this book, a number of techniques for doing this have been discussed. But key to all of these is a relationship between the adult and child. Parents and carers are very important in this. By using the skills of filial therapy, parents and carers can be empowered to work with and help their own children.

Filial therapy, an offshoot of play therapy, includes primary caregivers in the process of supporting the child. In filial therapy, the parents/carers act directly as the agents of therapeutic change, just as the therapist would do in non-directive play therapy. The play therapist works closely with the parents to teach them the necessary skills and techniques of non-directive play. Training and ongoing follow-up to support the parents/carers during the intervention can take a number of weeks to complete.

Filial therapy was developed by Bernard and Louise Guerney at Pennsylvania State University in the 1960s. The filial approach offers a structured training programme for prospective parents and carers in which they learn how to use child-centered play sessions or "special play times" at home. It is a well-established intervention, based in play, which can support, improve and/or reinforce the relationship between the child and the parent/carer. The filial therapy process preserves the principles of a non-directive approach. Being armed with child-centred play therapy skills to use with their children places parents – rather than the professional play therapist – back in the position of being the experts on and the healing agent for their children, and the benefits for the children are substantial.

Filial therapy has been well researched and evaluated (van Fleet, Ryan and Smith, 2005) and can lead to positive outcomes for children and enhanced family relationships. It requires practice and can be difficult so it is recommended that filial sessions happen only once a week for 20–30 minutes at a time for as many weeks as the parent and child want them. The shared play space can become very special for both as the parent witnesses the child's re-experiencing and move to mastery. Toys and resources used in these sessions should be kept separate from everyday toys. It is usual to practice filial therapy with the support and guidance of a play therapist trained in the method, and who may observe and then later discuss the interactions with the parent. You are assisting the child as they re-experience the arousal–relaxation cycle, the concept of which was so central to the work of Spaulding. In this re-experiencing, the child begins to learn that an adult *can* be trusted to be available to them, and self-esteem develops as they become aware that they are attended to and valued by the central person in their life – their attachment figure. This is why filial therapy is so powerful.

Filial therapy helps children and families

Generally, it is recommended that filial therapy play sessions take place at the same time and in the same place, preferably on a weekly basis. Therapy itself can usually take three–six months to complete; however, parents can continue to hold a weekly session with their child for as long as necessary, as long as their child wants.

Nina Rye (www.filialtherapy.co.uk) describes how filial therapy can help children to express their feelings and anxieties through the natural activity of play. She says that, over time, children may:

● 'Understand their own feelings better

● Become able to express their feelings more appropriately

● Be more able to tell parents what they need, what is worrying them

● Become more confident and skilled in solving problems as well as asking for help when they need it

● Reduce their problem behaviours

● Feel more secure and trust their parents more

● Have a more healthy self-esteem and increase their self-confidence.

Filial therapy can help parents to:

● Understand their child's worries and other feelings more fully

● Learn new skills for encouraging co-operation from their children

● Enjoy playing with their children and giving them positive attention

● Increase their listening skills and develop open communication with their children

● Develop self-confidence as parents

● Become more able to trust their children

● Deal in new ways with frustrations in family life'

(Reproduced with permission from www.filialtherapy.co.uk, accessed March 2009)

The underlying values of filial therapy reflect those discussed in Chapter 3 (Axlinian principles) but, more specifically, aim to provide an atmosphere of (van Fleet, 2008):

honesty
openness
respect, empathy, understanding and acceptance
genuiness
relationship
empowerment
humility
collaboration
playfulness and humour
emotional expression
family strengths
balance

Parents and carers can use the principles of filial therapy to enrich their relationship with their child. Children experiencing such intense synchrony and attunement respond well, because their attachment needs – for emotional resonance, empathic attention, soothing, stimulation, fun and attention – are all met by the person most important to them. Through this therapy, the child will soon learn to experience their parent as a fun, focused and empathic carer.

Although generally supported by a play therapist, a parent can learn and practise the five key principles of a play session. It can be difficult not to lead, teach, direct or ask questions, but once the adult begins to say what they see, and name what they believe the child is feeling, it becomes a valuable experience for both child and carer. Even using "attending" – a naming of feelings in day-to-day activities – gives the child the experience of "feeling felt" that was discussed earlier.

And if you get it wrong? Apologise to the child, acknowledge you got it wrong, and let the child correct you. This is empowering for children who may have distorted experiences of adult power.

We now explore the five key principles of empathic child-centred play.

The five aspects of a play session

Parents can be trained in sessions with the play therapist who teaches five principles of non-directive play, which are:

- Introducing the session
- Attending
- Reflecting feelings
- Setting limits
- Ending the sessions

Introducing the session

Enter the room – 'Amy…This is our special playtime and you can do almost anything you want in here. If there is something you can't do I will tell you…'

This is an important statement because the adult is being very clear that almost any behaviour is accepted in here but there are limits. Limits should be as wide as possible to give the child the freedom to experience and express as many emotions as possible but not so wide that the child feels unsafe and uncontained.

If children have experienced harm in their life then the play you witness may be distressing and you should be prepared for this. If you are in consultation with a play therapist, he or she will help you think about effective and attuned responses which will help your child re-experience the arousal–relaxation cycle talked about earlier. The other way you can help your child is by attending.

Attending

It is a rare experience to have someone closely attend to and focus on everything you say and everything you do with genuine curiosity and interest. You can let the child know that you are attending by being with them in the play space and noticing what they are doing, for example, look at the attending and empathic listening with Amy. Her carer was present and available but did not suggest, teach, direct or take control of the play. This may seem hard to do at first because it is not what adults are usually used to doing when

with children. This will be a new experience for you – and possibly for your child too. You will want to practise this skill and feel comfortable with it before trying the next key skill.

Reflecting feelings

Human beings experience a range of complex feelings. When children have experienced fear, loss and separation too early in their life, feelings get mixed up and it is hard to separate out one from the other. So, for example, for some children fear and excitement get confused – a child really looking forward to a birthday party, Eid, Diwali, Christmas or any event which is exciting or unfamiliar can confuse excitement with anxiety or even anger and will often appear to spoil the event by a tantrum or inappropriate behaviour. It is important to try to understand that the child is feeling emotions but often cannot name them. In play, children re-enact, if allowed to, their experiences and *feelings* and this is an opportunity for the child to name what they are experiencing – much as you would for a baby if you were soothing her. This will help the child to eventually recognise the feeling and *talk* about it instead of *act it out*.

Reflecting feelings takes a little practice but it is much like attending, except that you are attending to the *emotional* content of the play. Emotions are complex but the play can be kept simple and by using simple terms. Most children will understand the words "happy", "sad", "cross/angry", "scary", "yuck" – and you will know the words your child uses. For children who have not been predictably soothed or cared for, it is not knowing the word that is the problem – it is attaching the word to the right feeling!

Setting limits

Filial therapy helps adults set limits in a calm but firm and attuned way. A helpful way is to respond verbally immediately that the child wants to do something inappropriate, for example, throw something at you or paint on the walls. It is helpful to use her name and state what she cannot do – then offer an appropriate alternative. A helpful sentence to practise is:

> 'Jade – painting the wall is one of the things you can't do here but you can paint on this big sheet of paper.'